Following Mark

"With characteristic clarity and scholarly insight, William Loader takes his readers on an engaging step-by-step journey through the Markan text. The book's readable translations and informative explanations of individual sections will secure its place as a particularly reliable guide for those wishing to learn more about the meaning and significance of the Gospel of Mark."

—**Catrin H. Williams**, professor of New Testament studies, University of Wales Trinity Saint David

"William Loader's *Following Mark* distills the insights of a seasoned scholar and brilliant communicator into a highly readable format that will benefit those teaching or preaching the Gospel of Mark. This volume assists readers both to grasp the central message of Mark and to bridge the cultural gap back to the first-century world in which this text was written. Every page is replete with incisive and penetrating analysis of Mark's story of Jesus."

—**Paul Foster**, professor of New Testament and early Christianity, University of Edinburgh

"Bill Loader always writes with an open, inviting style that encourages thoughtful engagement with the biblical text. This short book is no exception. The pages brim with lucid explanations, vivid images, and provocative questions. Loader's own translation of Mark that is included is peppered with some wonderful turns of phrase that reflect how Australian ears hear the stories about Jesus. This book will help many as they read Mark's Gospel."

—**John Squires**, editor, *With Love to the World*

"*Following Mark* takes a fresh approach to the Gospel of Mark for preachers and all keen to develop their understanding of the New Testament. William Loader's clear and accessible explanation of nuances of translation, cultural and geographical contexts, and links to the Hebrew Bible provide the reader with a firm foundation for contemporary interpretation. This book will be invaluable for those faced with the challenge of reading and preaching the Scriptures in today's world."

—**Cathie Lambert**, formation and learning culture coordinator, Uniting Church Western Australia

"William Loader's deep knowledge of the text and its historical setting shines through in this immensely engaging and accessible introduction to Mark's Gospel. Written to be a concise guide for 'busy people,' this book is a superb resource for preachers, lay leaders, students, and all those who wish to learn more about following Jesus in the ancient world and in ours."

—**ROBYN WHITAKER**, associate professor of New Testament, University of Divinity

Following Mark

A Commentary for People on the Road

BY
William Loader

CASCADE *Books* • Eugene, Oregon

FOLLOWING MARK
A Commentary for People on the Road

Copyright © 2024 William Loader. All rights reserved. Except for brief quotations in critical publications or reviews, no part of this book may be reproduced in any manner without prior written permission from the publisher. Write: Permissions, Wipf and Stock Publishers, 199 W. 8th Ave., Suite 3, Eugene, OR 97401.

Cascade Books
An Imprint of Wipf and Stock Publishers
199 W. 8th Ave., Suite 3
Eugene, OR 97401

www.wipfandstock.com

PAPERBACK ISBN: 979-8-3852-0842-5
HARDCOVER ISBN: 979-8-3852-0843-2
EBOOK ISBN: 979-8-3852-0844-9

Cataloguing-in-Publication data:

Names: Loader, William R. G., 1944– [author].

Title: Following Mark : a commentary for people on the road / William Loader.

Description: Eugene, OR: Cascade Books, 2024.

Identifiers: ISBN 979-8-3852-0842-5 (paperback) | ISBN 979-8-3852-0843-2 (hardcover) | ISBN 979-8-3852-0844-9 (ebook)

Subjects: LCSH: Bible.—Mark—Commentaries. | Commentaries.

Classification: BS2585.53 L63 2024 (paperback) | BS2585.53 (ebook)

VERSION NUMBER 03/18/24

Contents

Preface | vii

Introducing Mark | 1

1 **The Beginning** | 4
    The Beginning of the Gospel (1:1–15) | 4
    Action! (1:16–45) | 12
    Jesus in Conflict (2:1—3:6) | 20
    Returning to Base (3:7–35) | 29
    Don't Give Up! (4:1–34) | 34
    Faith All at Sea (4:35–41) | 38

2 **The Expansion** | 41
    Israel and Beyond (5:1–43) | 41
    Confronting Rejection (6:1–29) | 47
    Abounding (6:30–56) | 53
    Overcoming Barriers (7:1—8:26) | 57

3 **The Identity** | 66
    Who Is He and Who Are We? (8:27—9:13) | 66
    Demons and Disciples (9:14–50) | 73
    Divorce, Remarriage, and Children (10:1–16) | 78
    Confronting Wealth and Poverty (10:17–31) | 83
    Wanting to Be Top Dogs (10:32–52) | 88

CONTENTS

4 **Jesus and the Temple** | 92
   Grand Entry? (11:1–10) | 92
   Jesus and the Temple Establishment (11:11–26) | 96
   Confrontations (11:27—12:44) | 101
   Predicting the Temple's Destruction and History's Climax (13:1–37) | 108

5 **The End?** | 114
   Jesus Facing the End (14:1–21) | 114
   Final Meal (14:22–25) | 120
   Denial and Trial (14:26–72) | 125
   Crucifixion (15:1–39) | 132
   Resurrection and Renewal (15:40—16:8) | 137

What Now after Listening to Mark? | 142

Preface

"I'm too busy. Can you just give it to me in a few words? Tell me the key things I need to know, no padding. And make it easy reading, please!" Over the past two decades I have tried to do this by offering short commentaries on the New Testament texts set in the Lectionary from Sunday to Sunday. Thousands worldwide use my website (billloader.com) as a resource. It has struck me that while it is good to have comments on set readings, a lot is to be gained by hearing the whole story, following Mark from beginning to end.

This book is about offering up-to-date scholarship and its key insights on Mark in concise and readable form for busy people who really want to know but don't have time to plough through the many fine lengthy commentaries currently available. In each section I supply my own translation of Mark which keeps close to the Greek text. I have used the New Revised Standard Version when citing other parts of Scripture.

Each section comprises two main parts, "Listening to Mark" and "Thinking about Mark." I have also designed it in a way that people who meet in groups to study Mark can dip into it and I have appended suggestive questions for reflection at the end of each section. The best question to start with in relation to all of them is: *What is new or significant for you in what you have just read?*

To listen to Mark carefully is to engage in a cross-cultural encounter—across nearly two thousand years! Sometimes that means acknowledging distance and difference and being honest about it. Demonology is not how we today understand illness or the weather. Their generation did pass away without their predictions being realized. There is a sense in which allowing distance sometimes makes it possible to see more clearly, certainly more than when we hold things too close to our eyes. Paradoxically, sensing distance can lead to sensing proximity, commonality. Challenges then, become just as eloquent and confronting now. That is why, in part, we make the effort to listen. My hope is that this book will help people engage and to find such engagement to be enriching.

I could fill pages expressing appreciation for the enrichment I have experienced from dealing with these texts and working with scholarly colleagues on them over the last fifty years. In this instance, I would also like to thank Cascade Books for enabling me to share in this way. Most especially, at a personal level, I thank my wife, Gisela, who has supported me throughout and has proofread this latest book.

William Loader

Introducing Mark

If we look for Mark in Mark's Gospel, we will not find him. He is nowhere to be seen. At most we find his name in the title. Someone attached the words "According to Mark" to a papyrus copy of Mark's Gospel in the decades following when it was written, probably on its wrapper. Mark or Marcus was a common name, but this Mark was someone special. It probably referred to John Mark, mentioned in Luke's account of the early church in the book of Acts (12:12, 25; 15:37). Was he the actual author? Or does it mean that the Gospel was written in a community that had a special connection with that Mark some time in the past? If you wanted to substantiate the authority of a gospel, it might have been better to pick someone less obscure. Very early, a story circulated according to which Mark acted as Peter's secretary, taking notes from Peter's sermons.

We may never know exactly who wrote the gospel attributed to Mark. The author—let us from now on call him Mark for the sake of simplicity—would probably have responded to our curiosity by saying: the author of the gospel is Jesus! The authors of the other three gospels in the New Testament would probably have answered similarly. All four gospels are anonymous. Their titles were all added later.

While we may never know who Mark the author really was, we are not left with nothing more to say. On the contrary, composing a gospel was an amazing achievement. Mark was an author with great skill. While it was clear that the baptism was at the beginning of Jesus' ministry, and the death at the end, the sequence of events in between was anything but clear. There was no diary or historical outline for Mark to work with. He had to arrange very diverse material into a single whole and make it into a single story. Matthew and Luke mostly followed his sequence of events, but also felt free to rearrange it sometimes, such as when Matthew brings together a sequence of typical actions of Jesus in chapters 8–9, some taken up from where they occur later in the story in Mark. Getting the arrangement right such that it made sense was a huge task.

Our Mark was therefore a highly skilled composer. It must have taken him a lot of time to develop his outline. We can see from his gospel that he must have had collections of stories that had already been passed on together over the four decades of the church's life. Thus we find a set of five stories in chapters 2–3 dealing with Jesus facing criticism and giving pithy two-liner responses. Similarly, it looks like people passed on parables about seeds in a cluster, now preserved in chapter 4. As we follow Mark, we shall find more examples of the way Mark had to integrate such collections from oral tradition into his story of Jesus.

It was not uncommon in the first-century world of Mark for authors to compose lives of famous people, biographies. Typically, they are told to highlight the person's significance, similarly drawing on anecdotes and collections of sayings, and sometimes doing so in a way that showed great creativity, such as putting together speeches and dialogues to fill out the story and underline the person's significance and sometimes creating symbolic narratives where events in the world of nature underline that significance. People learned to compose such stories as part of their education. It was an element of the study of rhetoric, that is, how to write speeches and stories that will engage and persuade an audience. Mark must have had such an education.

Like other such authors of his day, Mark wrote his gospel to be read aloud. To keep your audience with you, you had to employ rhetorical techniques. This included beginning and ending a section in a similar way so that people would sense it was a unit and recall its theme. Planning a composition such as a gospel was a major undertaking. Even getting it written down was complex. Usually, the author dictated it and someone else wrote it down. That would have taken a lot of time. The author would have to have an outline and notes. We can imagine that the whole process must have been a huge task that took not only days but weeks.

Mark would not have composed his gospel from scratch, making it up as he went along. We can imagine that he must have been part of a faith community meeting in his or someone else's house, where he will have told and retold stories and sayings of Jesus for many years. It was not as though he was inventing a story with which his hearers would not have already been familiar. In that sense he was simply putting into being a single sequence of stories and sayings that had been told and retold in scattered congregations of Christ-believers across the Mediterranean world for nearly four decades. Matthew and Luke knew this, and this is why, in using Mark as their basic outline a decade or so later, they also felt free to change the order and relocate episodes for better effect.

Clearly the time must have come when Mark made the decision to write it all down and put it all together. By the time he was writing, most if not all of the first generation had died and there was a need to preserve the tradition and secure it. This was all the more so because it could easily get out of control and people start making up stories and making new claims that went far beyond and sometimes far astray from what had been taught.

Thus, while we know next to nothing about the author, we surely do know that he was a skilled composer motivated to present Jesus to his world. Based on what he wrote and how he wrote (or had someone else write down), we also learn that he was familiar with Israel's traditions, in particular as we know them through the Old Testament. He must have assumed that his audience would include people familiar with biblical tradition. Perhaps some were Jews or gentiles (non-Jews) who had at some stage converted to Judaism. His audience certainly seems to include gentiles, for whom he offers explanations occasionally, but even many of them will have been familiar with Israel's traditions because they were often alluded to in anecdotes and stories about Jesus. Into which of these categories our author falls we may never know. I suspect the latter.

Let us then follow Mark, reading and reflecting on his gospel as he wrote it for his world and keeping an eye on what it might mean for ours.

1

The Beginning

The Beginning of the Gospel (1:1–15)

Listening to Mark

The beginning of good news story of Jesus Christ, the Son of God, was like this. ² As the prophet Isaiah put it, "Look, I am sending my messenger ahead of you, who will prepare your way, ³ a voice calling out in the wilderness, 'Prepare the way of the Lord; make his paths straight!'"

⁴ John came baptizing in the outback and announcing a baptism in which people could represent their turning to God and having their sins forgiven. ⁵ And the whole Judean region and all Jerusalem went out to him and were being baptized by him in the Jordan River, confessing their sins. ⁶ John wore a camel hair cloak with a leather belt around his waist and used to eat locusts and wild honey. ⁷ He proclaimed, "Someone is coming after me who is more powerful than me. I am not worthy even to untie the strap of his sandals. I baptize you with water; ⁸ but he is going to baptize you with the Holy Spirit."

⁹ And it happened in those days that Jesus of Nazareth in Galilee came and was baptized in the Jordan by John ¹⁰ and immediately having come up out of the water he saw the heavens torn open and the Spirit coming down into him like a dove. ¹¹ And a voice came from the heavens saying, "You are my beloved Son; I am very pleased with you."

¹² Then straightaway the Spirit sent him off into the outback. ¹³ And he was there in the outback for forty days having his mettle

tested in an ordeal with Satan and was there with the animals and angels looked after him.

¹⁴ After John was arrested, Jesus came to Galilee proclaiming the good news about God ¹⁵ and saying, "The time of fulfillment has arrived, and the kingdom of God has now come near. Turn to God and believe the good news!"

Thinking about Mark

Mark commences his gospel with the words, "The beginning of the good news story. . . ." The words, "the beginning," may have triggered for some the way the book of Genesis begins: "In the beginning. . . ." It would suggest to them that the story of Jesus is also sacred story.

The words, "the good news story," often simply translated, "the gospel," may seem very straightforward to us: this is the start of Mark's Gospel. There is, however, much more to it. Another way to translate the Greek word behind "gospel" is "good news." It is as though Mark is saying: "I want to tell you about some great news, and this is how it started." The term "good news" or "gospel" had been used in church language from early days. When they spoke of proclaiming "the gospel," "the good news," they meant the message about Jesus and the message he brought. Mark was simply filling that out in the form of a whole story. From then on, people used "gospel" also to refer to such a composition and so we speak of four "Gospels."

The word "gospel" or "good news" would have rung bells for listeners who knew Israel's traditions. It would remind them of Isaiah 52:7, "How beautiful upon the mountains are the feet of the messenger who announces peace, who brings good news, who announces salvation, who says to Zion, 'Your God reigns.'" It is very likely that Jesus drew upon this passage in describing his own role. He came to bring "good news," and that meant peace and salvation and God's reign, the kingdom of God, a favorite term in his preaching. While the prophet envisages hope for his own time, Jesus employs such language to speak of hope in his own time and, for Mark, that is also the good news of hope that he is presenting.

In Mark's world, the world of the Roman Empire, many people would have been familiar with the word "gospel" or "good news" used in another way, because they would have heard it used in Roman propaganda, where we sometimes find it preserved on stone inscriptions. Rome and Rome's emperor are the "good news"; they bring peace, make the world safe and the emperor is the son of God. Some of the first hearers of Mark's Gospel would have sensed that Rome's claims and the claims of their faith were competing. When Jesus used the term "good news" he sometimes spoke of "good news for the poor," referring to his own people, many of whom lived in poverty and exploitation at the hands of Rome and its representatives. Luke has Jesus begin his ministry by defining his own role in the words of Isaiah 61:1, "The Spirit of the Lord is upon me, because he has anointed me to bring good news to the poor" (4:18).

Mark's opening words, "The beginning of the good news story," find an echo in 1:14-15, "After John was arrested, Jesus came to Galilee proclaiming the good news about God and saying, 'The time of fulfillment has arrived, and the kingdom of God has now come near. Turn to God and believe the good news!'" This is typical of how authors begin and end sections to help hearers sense how sections belong together. We use paragraphs to indicate sections. More importantly, we see how Mark uses 1:14-15 to remind his hearers of the good news and to speak of it in terms of hope. As in Isaiah 52:7, cited above, we have not only the term "good news" but also the reference to God's reign, the kingdom of God. It is ultimately good news about God and God's action to bring fulfillment of hope.

If we go back to Mark's opening words, we see that Mark describes the "gospel," "good news," as the "gospel/good news story of Jesus Christ, the Son of God." There is no contradiction between "the good news of God" in 1:14 and "the good news story of Jesus Christ" in 1:1, because for Mark it is clear that the good news Jesus brings is ultimately about God and God's reign. It is also at the same time the good news about Jesus as well as the good news he brings.

"Jesus Christ, the Son of God" also means more than we usually suppose. "Christ" is not Jesus' surname, as though he was the son of Mr. and Mrs. Christ. "Christ" is the English form of the Greek word *Christos*, which means "Anointed." Its Hebrew equivalent comes through into English as "Messiah." In other words, when Mark refers to Jesus Christ, he includes the implication that Jesus fulfills the ancient Jewish hope that God would send a leader, like King David, thus a "Son of David," to be the Anointed One, God's chosen Messiah, to bring liberation for the people. Faith proclaimed that Jesus is that Anointed One, the Christ, the Messiah, to be enthroned as king. In circles where people were less aware of Jewish hopes for a Messiah, "Christ" did eventually come to be seen as simply a second name, like a surname.

Kings, who acted on God's behalf on earth, were also hailed as God's sons at their coronation. Thus in Psalm 2 we read: "I will tell of the decree of the Lord: He said to me, 'You are my son; today I have begotten you'" (2:7). So Jesus is not only "Jesus Christ," but also "the Son of God." Some would have heard that as belonging to his role as the Messiah, but for others "Son of God" might mean much more. They would not have thought of it in a physical sense, as though God had a child, but there were rich notions in the world of the time, both in Judaism and in wider circles, that people might be hailed as God's representatives, such as when Roman emperors were called "sons of the gods," but also when someone was seen as a bearer of God's Spirit or even as an embodiment of God's wisdom. As we shall see, Mark underlines for his readers that Jesus is indeed at least God's agent and representative and stands in a unique relationship to God while remaining fully human.

Where did it all begin? According to John's Gospel, it began with Jesus as the Word before the beginning of creation. According to Matthew and Luke, who tell miraculous stories of Jesus' birth, recalling similar legendary stories about the birth of great heroes in ancient biographies, it began with Jesus' conception and birth. In Mark, it began with John the Baptist and Jesus' baptism by John. The information we have about Jesus stems primarily from his ministry, which began with John's baptism and lasted, according to Mark, but also Matthew and Luke, just one year.

To introduce John, Mark cites two Old Testament prophetic texts which he has loosely merged together. "As the prophet Isaiah put it, 'Look, I am sending my messenger ahead of you, who will prepare your way, a voice calling out in the wilderness, "Prepare the way of the Lord; make his paths straight!"'" In fact, Mark's quotation combines Malachi 3:1 with Isaiah 40:3-4, which begins with the words "the voice. . . ." Matthew and Luke correct Mark at this point by omitting the Malachi passage.

Mark uses words of hope from another era to speak of the coming of hope in Jesus and of John the Baptist's role in how it began. Mark tweaks the citation from Isaiah so that it now refers to the voice crying out in the wilderness—to match John's location—whereas originally the exhortation in Isaiah was that the way itself should be made in the wilderness. By portraying John as also fulfilling the prophetic hopes, Mark is connecting both John and Jesus to the stories of God's activities in the past. It was another way of saying: what I am about to report is part of the sacred story of God's dealing with human beings.

John's location in the wilderness, the outback, is also making a connection with the past. Israel, rescued from Egypt, made its way through the wilderness for forty years and then was able to enter the promised land. Movements for hope and change often made the wilderness their base, partly because it was safe and partly also because of its symbolism: they would soon enter the land and bring about change. Josephus, the Jewish historian, writing in the late first century CE, mentions John among the leaders of such groups.

Preparing oneself for sacred rites and generally for daily living meant washing, including immersing oneself in water. It was not about hygiene but reflected beliefs that some things such as bodily discharges made you unfit to enter holy places without undergoing purification. People understood this as a way of cleansing themselves from what were deemed to be ritual impurities, many of which, such as menstrual blood or seminal emission in sexual intercourse, had nothing to do with sin. They were simply natural human experiences that needed such ritual attention.

On the other hand, immersing oneself could also be connected with wanting to be cleansed from sin. This was how John used it, calling people to immerse in water, confessing their sins and seeking forgiveness. He was, however, innovative in requiring that people not immerse themselves, the usual practice, but have him immerse them. He immersed them in the Jordan River as a sign that it was God who forgave and cleansed people from sin. The fact that he did it to others, instead of leaving them to do it for themselves, gave him the nickname "the Dipper" or "Immerser," which we usually hear as "the Baptizer" or "Baptist" and so easily miss its intent. He dipped people in the Jordan, inviting people to let themselves be forgiven and cleansed by God.

John the Baptist called all to turn to God and receive God's forgiveness. Sometimes people overlook this when they reduce the Christian message to forgiveness of sins, as though that was the main good news that Jesus brought. Seeing his death as like a sacrifice for sins helped contribute toward such thought. Some even claimed that therefore forgiveness of sins was available only after Jesus' death. That ignored John the Baptist and also Jesus, himself, who offered forgiveness of sins in God's name already during his ministry. God's forgiveness had always been open to people in Israel's faith. There were many ways of speaking about forgiveness, including by referring to John, to Jesus' actions during his ministry, and to the impact of his death. They were all ways of declaring God's forgiveness. The fact that

John already offered God's forgiveness to all alerts us to the fact that Jesus' message was about much *more* than forgiveness, certainly as Mark presents it and as John the Baptist goes on to indicate.

John's dress and lifestyle was typical of the ancient prophets. Mark portrays him therefore as a prophet preparing the way for something, indeed someone greater to come. Accordingly, Mark has John declare: "Someone is coming after me who is more powerful than me. I am not worthy even to untie the strap of his sandals. I baptize you with water; but he is going to baptize you with the Holy Spirit" (1:7-8). By the time that John's Gospel was written, a few decades later, we see signs that there was a sense of rivalry between the movement of Jesus' followers and those who followed John. John's movement developed over the centuries into the Mandaeans, who are strongest today in modern-day Iraq. Mark shows no sign of such rivalry, nor does he see any problem in depicting Jesus as wanting to be immersed in God's grace, but he makes it very clear that, though John seems the senior in baptizing Jesus, he is in fact the junior preparing for Jesus, who was greater. Matthew even has John say so himself when he hesitates to baptize Jesus, only to be told that it was right that he should proceed (3:14-15).

John speaks of his baptizing with water and contrasts that with Jesus, who was to baptize with the Holy Spirit. This is our first hint about what was to be new about Jesus' ministry. He, too, would offer forgiveness of sins, but his distinctive role was that he would baptize with the Spirit. Within our church lectionary year, we most naturally might think that the reference is to the Day of Pentecost, when, according to Luke in Acts 2, the Holy Spirit descended upon the faithful. If that were so here, it would be very strange, because it would not be referring to Jesus' ministry at all but something that followed it. Rather, Mark is having John tell us about Jesus' ministry. In it he will, as it were, flood/baptize his world with the Holy Spirit, or, put more simply, he will by the Spirit enter the land and bring healing and renewal. Later, in 3:28-30 Jesus challenges his critics who say he is in league with evil spirits by declaring that his actions are made possible by the Spirit and to say otherwise is to blaspheme against the Spirit.

The emphasis on the Spirit as the power of Jesus' ministry fits well with the verses that follow in which Mark tells us that when John baptized Jesus, two major events occurred. First, the sky was torn apart and the Spirit came down into Jesus like a dove and, second, the voice of God was heard declaring him his Son (1:11). Hearers knowing the prophetic tradition would hear an echo of Isaiah 64:1, where the prophet cries out: "O that you would tear open the heavens and come down." In a universe that assumed the earth is flat and God and the heavens are above the sky, this was a way of saying: God is involved here. God has sent the Spirit.

Mark has, in that sense, created a highly symbolic scene. Perhaps the dove recalls the new beginning after the great flood, when Noah sent out a dove (Gen 8:8). Luke makes it even more vivid by having the Spirit descend in bodily form as a dove and alight on Jesus. First-century people recognized and appreciated such symbolic scenes. In Luke's Pentecost scene, he even has tongues of fire appear on people's heads and has a mighty rushing wind blow, reflecting the range of meaning of the Greek word for Spirit, which can also mean wind and breath.

The voice from heaven also belongs to the symbolic scene and echoes Mark's opening verse, which described Jesus as Son of God. It is the voice of God who declares from above: "You are my beloved Son; I am very pleased with you" (1:11). Again, as in the introduction to John, Mark has merged allusions to Old Testament texts. One is from Psalm 2:7, "You are my Son." The other is from Isaiah 42, which reads: "Here is my servant, whom I uphold, my chosen, in whom my soul delights; I have put my spirit upon him" (42:1).

The word for "servant" in Isaiah 42:1 could also be translated "child," bringing the connection with Psalm 2:7 even closer than at first appears. Some see in the word "beloved" an allusion to Isaac, Abraham's beloved son, sometimes seen as having the same impact as a sacrifice, though having been spared, and speculate that Mark may mean us to think of Jesus' death as a sacrifice here. More likely, Mark uses "beloved" to capture what was said in Isaiah 42, namely that God's servant/son was chosen and special.

It is typical of ancient writings to inform hearers right from the beginning of what they need to know about the story to follow. Now they know: Jesus is God's chosen one, God's Son, empowered by the Spirit to do God's work in the world. Some among Mark's hearers may have taken even more from this scene. For they, too, will have been baptized and they, too, will have celebrated receiving the Spirit and being adopted as God's children at their baptism. And they, too, are commissioned and empowered by the Spirit to share the mission of Jesus in their world.

Mark has the Spirit pull Jesus back into the outback regions for forty days. The forty days connects to Israel's forty years in the wilderness. Matthew and Luke know a version of this wilderness stay that lists three temptations. They echo Israel's temptations in the wilderness. Mark simply says

Jesus was tested. Mention of wild animals may indicate that Mark wants us to think of Adam and Eve being tested in the garden of Eden. Jesus is safe with these animals apparently. Whereas Adam and Eve failed their test, Jesus did not. Angels looked after him, as Mark imagines it. In Mark's world it was common to depict great people facing challenges to test their mettle before they embarked on major undertakings.

Mark has Jesus begin his ministry after John was arrested, unlike in the Gospel according to John, where for a while they operated at the same time (3:22–30). Sometimes we cannot know what is history and what is construction or imagination. John sometimes preserves useful historical information while at the same time being much freer in creating speeches and dialogues that have little historical value for reconstructing Jesus' ministry. John's depiction of a three-year ministry, for instance, might be more accurate than Mark's one year and John's dating of Jesus' death to the Day before Passover rather than on Passover Day may be more accurate. We might never know for sure.

The opening passage in Mark's Gospel comes to a climax with Jesus embarking on his ministry. He leaves the wilderness, the place of preparation and testing, and heads into Galilee, proclaiming the good news of God; the time of fulfillment has come; God's reign is just around the corner. Like John the Baptist, Mark has Jesus challenge people, therefore, to repent, that is, to change and turn to God and believe this good news. The call is not about believing an idea, but about opening oneself to be involved. What the breaking in of God's reign means becomes clear as we read the rest of Mark's account. Get involved!

Reflection: What was good about the good news then and what remains good about it now? What might Mark have meant in having John define Jesus' role as baptizing with the Spirit?

Action! (1:16-45)

Listening to Mark

Passing along the shore of the Sea of Galilee, he saw Simon and Andrew, Simon's brother, casting their nets out on the lake, for they were fishermen. [17] And Jesus said to them: "Come and follow me and I will turn you into people who fish for people!" [18] Straightaway they left their nets and followed him. [19] And going on a little further he saw James the son of Zebedee and John his brother and they were mending their nets in their boat. [20] And straightaway he summoned them. And they left their father in the boat with their workers and went off to follow him.

[21] And they came into Capernaum and immediately on the Sabbath he entered the synagogue and was teaching. [22] And they were amazed at his teaching because he was teaching them as one who had authority and not like the scribes. [23] And immediately there was a man in their synagogue with an unclean spirit and it cried out: [24] "What have you got to do with us, Jesus of Nazareth? Have you come to destroy us? I know who you are, the Holy One of God." [25] Jesus then rebuked it, saying, "Be quiet and come out of him!" [26] And the unclean spirit convulsed him and with a loud cry came out of him. [27] Everyone was so amazed that they discussed among themselves: "What is this? A new teaching with authority. And he gives orders even to unclean spirits, and they obey him." [28] And his reputation suddenly spread far and wide in all the region of Galilee.

[29] Straight after leaving the synagogue, they came to Simon and Andrew's house along with James and John. [30] Now Simon's mother-in-law was sick with a fever. And so they told him about her straightaway [31] and he approached her, took hold of her hand and lifted her up and the fever left her and she set about serving them.

[32] When evening came and the sun was setting, people brought to him all their sick and those possessed by demons [33] and the whole city turned up at the door. [34] He healed many who were sick with

various illnesses and exorcised many demons, forbidding them to say anything because they knew who he was.

[35] And very early next morning while it was still dark, he left and went out into an isolated place and was praying there, [36] but Simon and those with him chased him up [37] and finding him, said: "Everyone is looking for you." [38] He says to them, "Let's go elsewhere to the towns round about so that I can preach there, because that's why I've come."

[39] And he went out into their synagogues in all of Galilee, preaching and exorcising demons. [40] And a leper comes to him calling out to him, "If you are willing to do so, cure me." [41] And feeling angry [or: compassionate], he reached out his hand and touched him and said, "I will. Be cured!" [42] And straightaway the leprosy left him, and he was cured. [43] And Jesus immediately sent him off, sternly [44] instructing him, "See you tell no one anything about this, but go and show yourself to the priest and make the offering required in the law of Moses, as evidence for them." [45] But he went out and began to blab all about it and spread his reputation so that he could no longer enter town openly, but stayed in the outback areas and people kept coming to him from all over.

Thinking about Mark

In his opening section, 1:1–15, Mark tells us who Jesus is, what task confronts him (to baptize with the Spirit), how he is equipped for it (receiving the Spirit), and how he prepared himself. Now Mark is ready to report some of the things that Jesus did. Already in 1:14–15 Mark gives us a summary: "Jesus came to Galilee proclaiming the good news about God." In this way these verses not only round off the first section, but also introduce the next, a common pattern in rhetoric of the time.

Now Mark moves to action. It is very significant that the first action that Mark details is about Jesus asking others to join him, to be involved. He sees Simon and Andrew fishing in Lake Galilee and calls them: "Come and follow me and I will turn you into people who fish for people!" (1:17). As simple as that! Jesus was enlisting their help. He was not a loner. A little further on, he calls James and John also to join him. Later, Mark will show Jesus sending such followers out to do what he had been doing (6:7).

It is important to see that Mark does not picture Jesus saying: "follow me and admire and worship me," as though he was creating a fan club and concentrating on himself. Sometimes church language about Jesus makes it sound like that was his ambition. On the contrary, joining Jesus meant joining with him in his task, it was partnership and action under his leadership.

The image of fishing can also be easily misunderstood. Are people just numbers, fish to catch, on a recruitment drive to boost the movement's strength? At worst, some forms of mission seem to be a numbers game, also a strategy for boosting the budget. For Mark, fishing for people is about taking people seriously as people and challenging them to turn and be involved in partnership and action, to become good news and bearers of good news.

Mark tells other stories about Jesus challenging people to follow him, like Levi in the next chapter. We are used to speak of "following" Jesus as a way of being a Christian. Mark's story indicates that for Simon and Andrew, and James and John, it was something much more radical. Mark tells us that Jesus really did challenge some people to up and leave their work and their families. That was extreme. He was inviting them to step outside the economic and social system of the day, which held people in their place and gave them stability. Stepping outside the system meant becoming unemployed. It meant traveling in a group with Jesus from town to town and becoming entirely dependent on the generosity of sympathizers who might offer you a bed and some food. This was extreme behavior.

Much more than just an invitation to be partners, this was making a statement, a protest, about society in Galilee, where the social system benefitted some and kept others poor and exploited. That was life in Rome's empire as it played itself out in Galilee and elsewhere. Rome's agents, like Herod Antipas in Galilee, ruled, and beneath them were rich locals, mostly landowners, and under them were peasants, and the system was designed through its structure of dependence to keep everything in control, which effectively meant that the rich stayed rich and poor remained poor. Jesus confronted the empire or kingdom of Rome with the empire or kingdom of God. His movement was a protest against what was going on and a modeling of a different way where God's Spirit brought change and hope and healing.

In Galilee it worked having some followers give up their livelihoods because there were enough people who were not so desperately poor. There could be support. The group could assume it would survive and survive it did. Among those who came under the impact of Jesus only a minority were called to give up everything. Jesus told most people to stay where they were but commit themselves just as much to the vision of change and transformation. These residentials would have been the larger number and they were also crucial to enable those on the road with Jesus to survive.

The pattern of residentials and itinerants remained characteristic of the Jesus movement. When it began to spread far and wide, the itinerants became the visiting preachers and apostles who founded and then offered support to the locals. The locals, the residentials, became more and more important, as the center for activity and outreach in their locality, and the itinerants took on the role of visiting resource people, dependent on the locals for their survival, in that sense like ministers with stipends. Practical concerns changed that pattern over time, sometimes against conservative resistance, such as when Paul decided it would be helpful if he worked part time occasionally to relieve locals of the burden, contrary to the instruction Jesus gave his disciples (1 Corinthians 9). Paul never saw such instructions as irreversible rules that would stand against more caring options in different circumstances.

By starting his stories of Jesus' ministry with the call to these fishermen, Mark was making it very clear that Jesus was not intent on being a lone hero. He was building a team. One can imagine the first hearers of Mark's Gospel reflecting on the fact that they, too, were called to partnership, even when most of them would need to live out that radical commitment to God's empire and kingdom right where they were, a call that remains as relevant now as it was then.

Having reported Jesus' partnership initiative, Mark moves on to day one. It begins in the Capernaum synagogue and starts and finishes by referring to Jesus' authority: "And they were amazed at his teaching because he was teaching them as one who had authority and not like the scribes" (1:22); "Everyone was so amazed that they discussed among themselves: 'What is this? A new teaching with authority. And he gives orders even to unclean spirits, and they obey him'" (1:27).

Mark focuses on two aspects: Jesus' teaching and his control over unclean spirits. He offers no further detail about what Jesus taught, but it is natural to assume that he means that Jesus taught what, according to 1:14–15, he had been proclaiming across Galilee. We have to wait till chapter 2 before we can see why Mark contrasts his authority with that of the scribes. There, the theme of authority and of Jesus' new teaching returns and clearly relates to his approach to interpreting biblical law.

In contrast, the episode demonstrates Jesus' authority in relation to what Mark calls "unclean spirits." It takes us into a strange world very different from our own. The "science" behind talk of "unclean spirits" is what we understand as a myth. According to the myth, some angels looking down at the earth saw human women, found them sexually attractive, came down to earth and slept with them (probably implying: raped them). The women became pregnant and gave birth to giants. The giants fought each other to death and out of their corpses came half-human half-divine spirits, the unclean spirits, who then spread out across the earth causing havoc.

Genesis 6 mentions the myth very briefly, but in other writings, such as "The Book of the Watchers" in 1 Enoch 6–16, reflecting storytelling going back to the fourth century BCE, there is much more detail. One version of the story gives the spirits the names of illnesses. They are like personalized viruses that afflict humanity. This "science" explains misfortune, but especially physical and mental illness, as caused by these demons. To heal people, you needed to expel their demons. You could do so by addressing the demons directly or by various actions, such as touch or using substances. Sometimes, where it was a case of mental illness, people might cry out and appear to be possessed, as though taken over by an evil spirit or evil spirits.

In our world, we understand pathology differently. We do not personalize viruses; nor do we explain mental illnesses by attributing strange behavior to demon possession. Clearly, Mark operates with very different assumptions from our own. This was also true of Jesus, whose acts of healing and exorcism rest on assumptions we no longer share. Engaging Mark's story and also engaging who Jesus was means acknowledging such differences. They lived with many assumptions that we do not share, such as the belief that the universe was created around four thousand years before their time, that the earth was flat, and much else.

It is very clear that when Mark has Jesus speak of God's reign breaking in during Jesus' ministry, he is referring to Jesus' acts of healing and exorcism that liberated people from what oppressed them. Putting this episode up front illustrates how central this was in Mark's understanding of Jesus. Some people simply ignore the data and concentrate on other aspects of Jesus, sensing that it is not possible for us to find any connection with healing and exorcism today. Others practice a kind of deceit, never acknowledging that it was so.

It is healthy, however, to face up to the major difference between our world and theirs. For it can at the same time lead to us to find points of connection. One point of connection that we can hold in common with Mark and Jesus is that the underlying concern is to liberate people from the powers that oppress them. In their day they saw the need for such liberation at a number of levels, from the individual to nations. They saw nations as also under the power of demonic forces. We see no such thing, but we can embrace the notion that liberation, setting people free from what oppresses them, can apply in our time just as much to political powers as to individuals.

When Jesus proclaimed the coming of God's reign, he was implicitly criticizing Rome's reign as he saw it, so that hope for him entailed major transformation, which would bring peace and justice and create a caring society. This is even more apparent when we recognize that the word "kingdom" used in his favorite term for hope ("the kingdom of God") was also the word that could be translated "empire."

In Mark's opening episode on Jesus' ministry, the man with the unclean spirit accosts Jesus: "What have you got to do with us, Jesus of Nazareth? Have you come to destroy us? I know who you are, the Holy One of God" (1:24). Mark and Mark's hearers would have recognized these words as coming from the unclean spirit, who speaks on behalf of his fellow demons. The assumption is also that the demons would recognize who Jesus was and what he could do. He was God's "Holy One," as Mark's hearers know already from earlier in the chapter, and he had the power to destroy them. Victory of the demonic forces was central to Jewish hope at the time. It was hope for liberation.

By depicting the unclean spirit as speaking in this way Mark is reinforcing for his hearers who Jesus was and what he could do. He is the agent of liberation. We shall find further references to Jesus' confrontation with the demons later in Mark, including when in response to another confrontation he sends them into pigs who rush off to drown in the Sea of Galilee.

Mark's story moves on to Simon (Peter) and Andrew's house, where they, along with James and John, find Simon's mother-in-law ill with a fever. They tell Jesus, who promptly takes her by the hand and lifts her up and the fever subsides. When Luke retells the story, he adds that Jesus addressed the fever, reflecting the assumption that an unclean spirit had brought the fever. The what and how of the healing is for us obscure and hard to believe.

Mark then reports that by evening large crowds had gathered and that Jesus "healed many who were sick with various illnesses and exorcised many demons" (1:34). He adds "forbidding them to say anything because they knew who he was," as did the unclean spirit in the man in the synagogue. Jesus was engaging in acts of liberation. This is what baptizing people with the Spirit, as John had described his mission, entailed. This was the kingdom of God, God's reign, beginning to show itself.

In Mark's storyline, day two follows. It reports that Jesus rose early and withdrew to an isolated place to pray (1:35). Simon and his friends chased him down, telling him that people were looking for him. Mark has Jesus indicate that he has other priorities, namely, to visit other towns, teaching in their synagogues and doing exorcisms.

Mark portrays the disciples as not really in tune with Jesus' priorities. Perhaps he means us to see them as concerned with Jesus' popularity. Perhaps he means simply to portray them as limiting their priorities to the local scene and not seeing the bigger picture. Certainly, Mark will have been placing value on Jesus' withdrawal to pray and on not simply responding to every need, a piece of wisdom of abiding relevance for all who work to deal with people in need. That sometimes means needing to set priorities in the light of wider needs and sometimes to say, no.

Mark's timeline moves now beyond just those first two days as he portrays Jesus fulfilling his commission in the region (1:39). The final incident in Mark 1 reports Jesus' encounter with a leper (1:40–45). What they then described as leprosy appears to have been different from Hansen's disease, the form that leprosy takes as we know it. They were referring to a contagious skin disease that required that people isolate, recalling for us what became a mandate during the COVID pandemic. Biblical law set down rules about isolation and also about being declared no longer contagious.

The description of Jesus' initial response to the man's approach varies among the manuscripts of Mark. Some say Jesus was angry. Others say he was moved with compassion. People were more likely to change anger to compassion than the reverse. If anger is original, it was because in doing so the man broke the law and endangered Jesus and those around him. Whatever Jesus' immediate emotional response might have been, his considered response was to set aside the danger to himself, touch him, and heal him, and then urge him to remain quiet about it, but go to the priests, who had authority to declare people no longer contagious, and make the required offering. The man did the latter but ignored the former, announcing to all what had happened, which resulted in Jesus being thronged, causing him to stay outside the towns. The crush of the crowd plays a role also in the next story in Mark's account.

Mark has not only given a picture of the disciples as not always being in tune with Jesus. He also indicates that those whom Jesus helped did not always prove helpful. Being thronged by adoring crowds was not Jesus' preference. In the broader context it could even bring danger, especially in a world where authorities looked on unrest and mass movements with suspicion. Mass movements have always posed a danger also in the sense that popularity so easily becomes the priority.

Mark will return in the following chapters to tell stories that throw more light on his earlier statement, that Jesus taught with authority and not as the scribes. Mark may well have placed the story of the leper's healing here to help hearers realize that Jesus observed what the biblical law required and urged the man also to do so. He was not disrespectful of biblical law. His conflict, as we shall see, was getting one's priorities right when interpreting it. Here, the biblical command not to touch a leper is overridden by the biblical command to care.

Reflection: What did following Jesus mean then and what does it mean now? How do we relate Jesus' ministry of exorcism to our current understandings of human need?

Jesus in Conflict (2:1—3:6)

Listening to Mark

2:1 And he came again into Capernaum some days later and people heard that he was at home. **2** And many gathered so that there was no longer room to move, not even at the front door, and he was giving them the message. **3** And they came bringing him a man who was paralyzed, being carried by four men. **4** And unable to get him to Jesus because of the crowd, they removed part of the roof over where he was and, digging it open, let down the stretcher on which he was lying. **5** When Jesus saw their faith, he said to the paralyzed man, "Son, your sins are forgiven." **6** Now some scribes were sitting there and they were tossing over in their minds: **7** "Why does this fellow speak like this? He's blaspheming. Who can forgive sins but God alone?" **8** And immediately sensing in his spirit that they were bothered about this, Jesus said, "Why are you upset about this? **9** What is easier, to say to the paralyzed man, 'Your sins are forgiven' or to say, 'Get up and take your stretcher and walk'? **10** But so that you may know that the Son of Man has authority on earth to forgive sins"—he says to the paralyzed man—**11** "I tell you, get up, pick up your stretcher and go back home." **12** And he got up, picked up his stretcher, and went on out in front of them all, so they were all amazed and glorified God, saying "We've never seen anything like this!"

13 And they set off again to the lakeshore and the whole crowd went to him and he was teaching them. **14** As he was going along, he saw Levi the son of Alphaeus sitting at the customs desk, and he says to him: "Follow me!" And he got up and followed him. **15** And it happened that when he was sitting in Levi's house, many toll collectors and sinners were sitting along with Jesus and his disciples. **16** And the scribes of the Pharisees, seeing that he was dining with sinners and toll collectors, were saying to his disciples, "Why is he dining with toll collectors and sinners?" **17** When he heard, Jesus says to them, "The well don't need a doctor; the sick do. I didn't come to summon the righteous, but sinners."

¹⁸ Now John the Baptist's disciples and the Pharisees were fasting, so they come and ask him, "Why do John's disciples and the Pharisees' disciples fast, but your disciples don't?" ¹⁹ Jesus responded to them, "The bridegroom's men can't fast while the bridegroom is with them. As long as he is with them, they can't fast. ²⁰ But the days will come when he will be taken away from them and then they will fast on that day. ²¹ No one sews a piece of unshrunk cloth onto an old garment; otherwise, the patch would pull away from it, the new from the old, and the tear would become worse. ²² And no one puts new wine into old wineskins; otherwise, the wine would burst the wineskins and both the wine and wineskins would be lost; but you put new wine into new wineskins."

²³ And it happened one day that they were wandering through a field of wheat and the disciples started plucking heads of grain as they made their way along. ²⁴ And the Pharisees were saying to him, "Look, why are they doing what is forbidden on the Sabbath?" ²⁵ He responded, "Haven't you read what David did when he faced need and was hungry along with his companions, ²⁶ how when Abiathar was high priest he ate bread set aside for offering, which only the priests are allowed to eat and also gave some to his companions?" ²⁷ And he was telling them, "The Sabbath was made for human beings not human beings for the Sabbath. ²⁸ So the Son of Man is master also of the Sabbath."

³:¹ And they came again into a synagogue and there was a man there with a shrunken hand. ² And people were watching him to see if he would heal him on the Sabbath, so that they might lodge a charge against him. ³ And he says to the man with the shrunken hand, "Come here into the middle." ⁴ And he said to them, "Is it lawful to do good or do harm on the Sabbath, to save life or to kill?" They kept silent. ⁵ And looking around angrily at them, aggrieved at their heartless attitude, he says to the man, "Stretch out your hand." And he stretched it out and his hand was restored. ⁶ And immediately the Pharisees plotted with the Herodians against him, how they could kill him.

Thinking about Mark

Mark 1 ended with a story showing Jesus' insistence on keeping biblical law and also the leper's defiance of Jesus' instruction to keep his healing quiet, resulting in Jesus being swamped with people wanting to see him and so needing to withdraw to outside the towns. In Mark's storyline this sets the scene for what follows in Mark 2. He comes home to Capernaum, where, apparently, he was living at the time, and the crowds surround his house (2:2), recalling what happened when he was in Peter's house where Mark says that "the whole city" had gathered at the door (1:33).

The few details invite us to imagine the scene. Houses were usually open to the street with only the private quarters in the back inaccessible. Crowds had pressed into the front space of the house and many more were outside the main door or gate. Mark tells us that Jesus was addressing them. We have to imagine what he was saying. From what we have heard so far in Mark, we can imagine that Jesus was speaking about God's reign and calling people to respond and become involved.

A drama unfolds. Four men carried a paralyzed man on a stretcher of some kind and found they were unable to make it through to Jesus because of the throng. So they climbed onto the roof above where Jesus was speaking, dug open a hole in the roof, which probably consisted of mud and wood supports, and let the man down (2:3-4). Detail is sparse. We do not know the man's name, his age, his origin, whether Jesus knew him previously, or what kind of paralysis he suffered from. It is typical of such anecdotes passed on by word of mouth that detail is trimmed to a minimum and all the emphasis falls on what Jesus says and does.

Jesus recognized the faith that the helpers were putting in him and said to the man: "Son, your sins are forgiven" (2:5). The underlying assumption is that his paralysis was somehow linked to his sins. Our understandings of paralysis would open a detailed discussion far beyond what first-century people would have assumed. They saw a connection between sin and paralysis, at least in some instances. We might consider it possible but rare. The story assumes it in this case.

Jesus picks up the fact that some of the scribes, religious teachers, in the crowd were troubled by what he said. Mark puts words into their mouths along the lines that their objection was that Jesus claimed to be able to forgive sins, usurping what was God's role alone. What authority did he have to do so! Mark's hearers would recognize that when Jesus declared the man's sins forgiven, he meant forgiven by God. Jesus was not acting independently of God. Similar problems had arisen with John the Baptist who effectively declared people's sins forgiven in the name of God when they repented and let themselves be immersed in the Jordan River, symbolic of letting themselves be immersed in God's mercy.

Jesus' response comes in the form of a confronting question: "What is easier, to say to the paralyzed man, 'Your sins are forgiven' or to say, 'Get up and take your stretcher and walk'?" (2:9). It is typical of responses we find in such anecdotes about Jesus in conflict. Usually, they are cleverly simple and have two parts or present two alternatives. At one level, it is much harder to ask someone to get up and walk than to tell them their sins are forgiven, but, of course, for Jesus' critics, it was much harder to hear the words, "your sins are forgiven," because they saw them as potential blasphemy.

The scribes do not come out well in the story. In some ways they are caricatures shown up as rather dumb. The story will have been told and retold to counter one of the objections brought against Jesus' later followers about their claims made for Jesus. The charge of blasphemy comes to a head in Mark's story of Jesus' trial before high priest in Jerusalem (14:63–64). Portraits of opponents are not always kind. Neither declaring God's forgiveness nor claiming to be a Messiah would have been originally seen as blasphemous, but such charges had gained currency by the time of Mark.

Assuming the anecdote preserves some memory of an actual event, the detail is scant, trimmed to a minimum. Usually, such anecdotes climax in a clever and challenging response by Jesus. As we shall see, the following four anecdotes in 2:13—3:6, follow the same pattern. They were probably remembered and passed on as a cluster of five stories and Mark has conveniently located them here in his storyline, as he will later bring a collection of parables about seeds, similarly remembered together, in Mark 4.

Mark weaves these five anecdotes together within his storyline and may well be responsible for some of the additional comments that now supplement Jesus' initial clever responses. This may well be the case in the first story where, before telling the man to get up, pick up his stretcher and go home, we read: "but so that you may know that the Son of Man has authority on earth to forgive sins . . ." (2:10). This recalls the theme of authority that Mark highlighted in the very first episode he recalls of Jesus' ministry (1:23–28).

Mark is making it clear that Jesus is God's agent, authorized to act on his behalf. In portraying Jesus as God's agent, Mark labels Jesus, "the Son of Man." The words could simply mean, "the human being," but clearly, they mean more than that here. In Jewish tradition it had become a pattern to depict history as a series of transitions between imperial powers, from the

Babylonians to the Persians, to the Greeks, and in Jesus' and Mark's time, the Romans, and to portray each as an animal, such as a lion, a bear, a leopard, or a goat. This is the pattern we find in the book of Daniel (7:1–28). History reaches its climax when a human being, "one like a son of man," ascends the throne and will act on God's behalf as judge.

In some circles, people identified this Son of Man figure with the royal Messiah, the Christ, the promised anointed king like David. Mark assumes this connection. Jesus is the Son of Man/Messiah, who will be the judge and who is authorized to act on God's behalf. This, then, makes sense of his claim here, as Son of Man, to be authorized to declare God's forgiveness. We find the close connection reappearing in Jesus' trial before high priest where, immediately after acknowledging that he was indeed the Messiah, Jesus goes on to speak of himself as the one who would come as Son of Man, with the clouds of heaven (14:62).

The second anecdote in Mark's collection of stories of conflict similarly relates to forgiveness, but in a different form (2:13–17). It begins with Jesus' call of Levi, a toll collector. His role was probably to collect customs duties from people moving across the boundary from the western side of the lake to the eastern side, such as from Bethsaida to Capernaum. Such toll or tax collectors had a reputation for overcharging and so exploiting travelers. If you listed notorious sinners, tax collectors would be among them. Just to challenge Levi to join him implied acceptance and forgiveness. We find him called Matthew in the gospel of the same name (9:9–13).

Levi must have invited Jesus and his disciples to join him for dinner along with others: "toll collectors and sinners." Even just to accept such an invitation and enter such a sinner's house was not the sort of thing one would expect of a man seeking to be holy. It would expose you to ritual impurities because you could never be confident that a sinner would observe biblical law. It will also potentially expose you to morally evil influences which were bound to be present in such bad company. The anecdote is one of many that highlight what people saw as Jesus' notorious behavior. Perhaps the most famous instance is the story that Luke brings of Jesus inviting himself to the house of Zacchaeus the tax collector (Luke 19:1–10).

Such toll collectors could afford to dine well and to make their meals occasions for entertainment. Behind the word "sinners" in the words, "toll collectors and sinners," we may imagine such entertainers, perhaps even local prostitutes. Dinners were frequently a preferred site not only for entertainment, but also for conversation and listening to guest teachers or orators. In the wider Mediterranean world such occasions could be called symposia, and many Greek philosophers composed works that imagined such a setting for dialogue and debate in presenting their ideas. Jesus was apparently prepared to fulfill the role of being such a guest.

In response to the criticism from some scribes of the Pharisees, Jesus gives a typically terse reply: "The well don't need a doctor; the sick do" (2:17). Behind this response are some important assumptions. There is sickness. There is need, including need for forgiveness and acceptance, and Jesus is there to offer it. More than that, offering such help is a higher priority than protecting oneself from moral or ritual contamination to which one might be subjected by such action. This assumes, in turn, that God's priority is care and concern, not remaining separate and aloof. The saying speaks of "the well," not in any way disparaging the well but challenging them to come on board with this concern.

Finally, whether original to Jesus or added subsequently, we hear words that seek to spell out that concern: "I didn't come to summon the righteous, but sinners" (2:17). He had called Levi. There is no intention to exclude "the righteous." Jesus reaches beyond them, while at the same time challenging them, especially his critics who consider themselves as righteous and are concerned to preserve that status, to look beyond themselves.

Mark has three more anecdotes to tell. This second one was about eating. The next one is about fasting and the one that follows is again about eating. Such patterning was typical of storytellers in the ancient world. In this third anecdote, 2:18–22, we find people noticing that, while the disciples of John the Baptist and those of the Pharisees practiced fasting, Jesus' disciples did not. Jesus' initial response uses marriage imagery to assert that his ministry is the time to celebrate. In a world of food scarcity or at least of very limited means, feasts such as wedding feasts played a major role. The previous anecdote reflects the fact that only those with money could afford special feasts and dining occasions.

One of the favorite ways of imagining future hope, the kingdom of God, was to picture it as a grand feast. Some saw it as for their group exclusively. Jesus spoke of it as a feast to which all are invited and sometimes referred to it as like a wedding feast. Here he makes the claim that already during his ministry the kingdom of God, God's reign, was breaking in. He is like the bridegroom; so let the celebrations begin! No need for fasting.

We find a number of other sayings attached to this anecdote. Immediately after the words about the bridegroom's presence and the appropriateness of celebration, we find reference to the bridegroom's absence. These words reflect on the time after the death of Jesus when members of the Jesus movement would engage in fasting and may reflect a supplementary addition to the anecdote.

The next two sayings about sewing unshrunk cloth onto an older garment and pouring new wine into old wine skins (2:21–22) take up the theme of newness which Mark introduces in the first episode of Jesus' public ministry: "What is this? A new teaching with authority" (1:27). The sayings serve Mark's purpose well. They may go back to Jesus. Mark brings them here to forge a contrast between two ways of interpreting biblical law. They highlight the conflict between the approach taken by Jesus' critics and that of Jesus himself. To treat them as a claim on the part of Jesus to abandon the biblical law and replace it with his own would be a misreading. Jesus and the Jesus movement is not to be tucked back into the traditional patterns characteristic of John and the Pharisees. The time of celebration, like celebrating a wedding feast, has come, a time for radical love reaching out to sinners as a mark of the new initiative, which belongs to the breaking in of God's reign.

The fourth and fifth anecdotes deal with conflict over the Sabbath. In 2:22–28 the objection from some Pharisees was that Jesus' disciples were plucking heads of wheat as they walked through a field and were eating them. A very extreme interpretation could argue that to pluck and roll the heads of wheat in your hands to remove the husks in order to eat the grains of wheat represented work and so contravened one of the ten commandments about not working on the Sabbath.

Jesus' typical two-part response was: "The Sabbath was made for human beings not human beings for the Sabbath" (2:27). In this way he shunted aside the issue of whether it was breaking the commandment or not and shifted the focus to humankind. At some stage the story received a supplementary argument about how David fed his men when they were hungry by having them eat what was preserved strictly only for the priests (1 Sam 21:1–7). It incorrectly dates the event to the time when Abiathar was high priest, something Matthew and Luke later correct (Matt 12:1–8; Luke 6:1–5). It also justifies the disciples' actions by implying that they were hungry and so Matthew changes the description of the event to portray the disciples as hungry.

It is possible that this explanation about David came from Jesus, but it seems more likely to be a secondary supplement. Matthew adds even more when he rewrites the anecdote, pointing to how priests work on the Sabbath (12:5) and then citing Hosea 6:6, "I desire mercy and not sacrifice" (12:7), one of two occasions where Matthew adds it (also in 9:13).

The impression given by Jesus in this anecdote, as in the previous three, is that God's priorities are not about having to keep particular rules but about focusing on people, whether in need or not. It is a more positive, open understanding of God. As in the first anecdote, Mark brings here a reference to Jesus and his authority as the Messiah/Son of Man: "So the Son of Man is master also of the Sabbath" (2:28). This is not to say: abandon Sabbath law and do only what Jesus says. Rather, it is to say: obey Sabbath law as Jesus interprets it.

The final anecdote (3:1–6) takes place in a synagogue and in that sense reminds us of the opening scene of Jesus' public ministry in 1:21–28. In this scene Jesus finds a man with a shrunken hand among those present. As usual, we are not told precisely what the problem was: a broken hand? A dupuytren's contracture? A limp hand? The focus here is on the need and whether Jesus would respond to it on the Sabbath—and so, work and thereby break the commandment, according to his critics. Mark portrays the critics as extreme and unreasonable, probably reflecting the way the story had functioned over the decades in warding off such criticism. Jesus' typically brief two-part response addressed directly to the man is: "Is it lawful to do good or to do harm on the Sabbath, to save life or to kill?" (3:4).

His critics might have argued: why don't you leave it till tomorrow to heal him? In the story Jesus is clearly not at all bothered by criticism. His focus is the man and his need there and then. He could have suggested leaving it for a day but is not shown as concerned to do so. Again, the contrast with his opponents appears to be that they were concerned about strict observance and that Jesus took a more liberal approach, in this case not seeing any reason to postpone healing action.

The alternative: "to do good or to do harm on the Sabbath" is provocative and would, one imagines, have annoyed his critics. The second contrast, perhaps a supplement, has a sharper edge and goes beyond the scene: "to save life or to kill." Healing a hand is a long way from saving a life. This second alternative seems designed to introduce reflection on what follows. After reporting the healing and Jesus' being aggrieved at their stubbornness, Mark adds: "And immediately the Pharisees plotted with the Herodians against him, how they could kill him" (3:6). As in the charges of blasphemy in the first anecdote, so here, too, Mark points forward to Jesus' fate.

The linking of the Pharisees and the Herodians is unusual. The Herodians are authorities associated with Herod Antipas, ruler of Galilee under the Roman Empire. Ultimately it will be the Roman administrative authorities, namely Pilate, who will execute Jesus. A collusion between Pharisees and the ruling authorities would be unusual and certainly would be seen by Mark's hearers as putting Pharisees in a bad light. In the end we find no involvement of Pharisees in Jesus' execution, but they certainly played a role as opponents of the Jesus movement in the early decades of the church.

Reflection: What does Mark portray as the issue in understanding God's priorities and how do you see such conflicts playing out in faith communities today?

THE BEGINNING

Returning to Base (3:7–35)

Listening to Mark

$^{3:7}$ Jesus and his disciples set off for the lake and a great crowd from Galilee followed him; and from Judea, ^{8} Jerusalem, Idumea, the Transjordan, and the regions around Tyre and Sidon, also a great mob of people came when they heard what he was doing. ^{9} And he told his disciples to get a boat ready for him because of the crowd so that they would not crush him, ^{10} for he healed many and as a result people with afflictions pushed toward him, wanting to touch him. ^{11} Unclean spirits, when they saw him, fell down before him and shouted out, "You are the Son of God," ^{12} and he had to tell many of them off, to stop them making known who he was.

^{13} Then he goes up a mountain and calls those he wanted to join him to come, and they joined him. ^{14} And he appointed twelve whom he designated as apostles to be with him and whom he could send out to preach ^{15} and have power to expel demons. ^{16} So he appointed the twelve. He gave Simon the name Peter, ^{17} and James the son of Zebedee and John, James' brother, the name Boanerges, which means sons of thunder. ^{18} He also appointed Andrew, Philip, Bartholomew, Matthew, Thomas, James the son of Alphaeus, Thaddeus, Simon the Cananaean, ^{19} and Judas Iscariot, who betrayed him.

^{20} He comes home and again a crowd gathers so that they were scarcely able to eat. ^{21} When his family heard, they went out to restrain him because they were saying he was beside himself. ^{22} And scribes from Jerusalem had come and were saying he was possessed by Beelzebul and was casting out demons with the help of the prince of demons. ^{23} So he summoned them and addressed them in parables saying, "How can Satan cast out Satan? ^{24} If a kingdom is divided against itself, that kingdom cannot stand ^{25} and if a household is divided against itself, that household cannot stand. ^{26} And if Satan rises up against himself and is divided, he cannot stand but that's the end of him. ^{27} But no one can enter a strong man's house to plunder his goods, unless he first ties the strong man up and then he will plunder his house. ²⁸ Truly, I tell you, everything can be forgiven human beings, including the blasphemies they utter, ²⁹ but whoever blasphemes against the Holy Spirit will never receive forgiveness but is guilty of an eternal sin." ³⁰ For they were saying that he had an unclean spirit.

³¹ His mother and brothers came and were standing outside and sent for him, summoning him. ³² And a crowd was sitting around him, and they tell him, "Look, your mother and brothers and sisters are outside wanting you." ³³ But in response he says to them, "Who are my mother and my brothers?" ³⁴ And looking around at those seated round about him, he says, "Look, my mother and my brothers! ³⁵ Whoever does the will of God, they are my brother and my sister and my mother."

Thinking about Mark

Mark began his account of Jesus' public ministry with a twofold focus: Jesus as healer and exorcist and Jesus as teaching with authority. In the rest of Mark 1 he illustrated Jesus' activity as healer and exorcist. Then in Mark 2:1—3:6 he has demonstrated Jesus' teaching with authority in the context of conflict. Mark returns to a summary statement in 3:7-12 about Jesus' healing activities and the crowds that came to him, causing him to seek the safety of boarding a boat close to shore. As before (1:24, 34), the unclean spirits whom he was casting out recognized him as Son of God, but he sought to silence them.

In Mark 3:13-19, Mark cycles back to speak of disciples, as he had done in 1:15-20. He will return to them a third time in 6:7-13, when he describes their commissioning. Now, in 3:13, he has Jesus ascend a mountain and summon his chosen disciples. Matthew will pick up this brief reference and use it to introduce his first extended summary of Jesus' teaching, the Sermon on the Mount (Matthew 5–7). Mark focuses on the appointment of twelve disciples. Mark's hearers would recognize the symbolism of Israel with its twelve tribes. Mark has Jesus call them "apostles," that is, envoys who will go out "to preach and have power to expel demons" (3:14-15), in other words, to do what Jesus was doing and so expand its impact. Mark gives more information about their commissioning in chapter 6.

Simon comes first in the list and Mark indicates that Jesus gave him the nickname, "the Rock," in Aramaic "Cephas" and in Greek "Petros" or, as it comes through in English, Peter. Matthew plays with his name to have Jesus declare that he will make him the foundation rock of the church and give him administrative authority over it (16:17–19), a task Matthew's Jesus later assigns also to congregations (18:15–18). Luke reports a miraculous fish catch in association with Peter's initial call to be a disciple (5:1–11), but John's Gospel locates it after Jesus' resurrection (21:4–14). Early reports of Jesus' resurrection mention Peter as the first witness, in that sense, indeed, the foundation of the church (1 Cor 15:3–5; Luke 24:34; Mark 16:7). Mark says little about his status, symbolic and otherwise, and will show him to be a very fallible human being who under pressure will deny knowing Jesus.

Stories came to be told about all twelve in the list, but the leading figures appear to have been Peter, James, and John. Judas became the outsider. The list mentions Matthew, apparently another name for Levi, whose call Mark reported. We might want to ask Mark about why he does not list others. The itinerant group also included women, like Mary Magdalene, who also played important roles at the end of Jesus' life and in the Easter stories. Luke mentions that some women were very important in providing financial support for the group (8:1–3). Alongside these, are all those followers who did not "follow" in the traveling group but stayed at home and committed themselves to the message of Jesus. And what about Jesus' family?

When Jesus returned home, the problem of crowds thronging him returned. "They could not even eat" (3:20) probably means that Jesus and his disciples were hemmed in. However, a more serious problem arose. Mark tells us about Jesus' family and what they were thinking. He does so by composing what some people call a sandwich structure in 3:20–36. It begins and ends with the theme of Jesus' family: 3:20–21 and 3:31–35. Sandwiched in between them in 3:23–30 is a report about scribes from Jerusalem who accuse Jesus of being in league with Beelzebul, one of the names of the chief of demons.

The passage is very confronting about Jesus' family. It begins by reporting the response to the predicament in which he found himself: "When his family heard, they went out to restrain him because they were saying he was beside himself" (3:21). This is the most natural rendering of the Greek and implies his family thought he was going mad. The scribes who alleged he was in league with demons were also effectively saying he was mad. Hence Mark's sandwiching together the similar accusations. A less disturbing translation, sometimes preferred, is to read: "people were saying" (as in the NRSV) instead of the more natural translation, "they [i.e., Jesus' family] were saying," as most translate it.

Mark shows no knowledge of the legendary stories of Jesus' birth where angels talk to Joseph or to Mary about baby Jesus. These are almost certainly later developments typical of biographies of famous people where authors imagined what miraculous births they must have had to turn out to be so famous. On the contrary, in Mark's story Jesus' family were a problem, as were many families when people joined Jesus' movement.

If we jump over to the end of this section where the family theme returns, we see the contrast of loyalties set out clearly for all to see. The crowds tell Jesus: "Look, your mother and brothers and sisters are outside wanting you" (3:32). His response was to point to those around him and declare that these were his family, adding, "Whoever does the will of God, they are my brother and my sister and my mother" (3:35).

Mark's failure to mention Joseph has people wondering: he may well have died. Assuming he might have been near thirty when Jesus was born, he would be have been sixty by the time Jesus commenced his ministry, an age that not many reached in those days.

A few chapters later, Mark portrays Jesus in his own home synagogue in Nazareth and those present observing, "Isn't this the builder's boy, Mary's son, and isn't he James and Joses and Jude and Simon's brother?" (6:3), to which Jesus responds by pointing out that traditionally prophets do not find acceptance among their own, including their own home and, by implication, his situation was no different (6:4).

Families then and now can wield enormous influence, which makes it difficult if that power is misplaced or misdirected. For some, purely at a personal level, they need to leave home to find themselves, in a sense to complete the birth process. Sometimes that entails serious psychological readjustment, dealing with what some might popularly call the demons within. A family's values may distort justice and promote destructive attitudes or narrow selfish interests, rather than the values of compassion and care, such as Jesus promoted. This was the case back then and is the case for many still today.

It is striking that Mark chose to insert the account of the scribes' accusations that Jesus was even worse than mad; he was an accomplice of Beelzebul, of Satan. Mark associates the family's assessment with the scribes' assessment. In those times, people attributed madness to demon possession but then to allege that Jesus derived his power from demons went much further. Jesus' response exposes the absurdity of their suggestion, because it implied demons acting against their own. More seriously, Jesus goes on to allow that people might engage in slander, including of himself, but to warn that to slander what he was doing through the power of the Spirit was in fact to slander God, which was unforgiveable, a distinction made even clearer in Matthew and Luke: "Whoever speaks a word against the Son of Man will be forgiven, but whoever speaks against the Holy Spirit will not be forgiven, either in this age or in the age to come" (Matt 12:32; similarly, Luke 12:10). The reference to the Spirit recalls John the Baptist's neat description of Jesus' mandate as to baptize with the Spirit (1:8).

Mark had begun his account of Jesus' ministry with an exorcism (1:21–28) and has returned to this theme in this section. It was a key element in Jesus' ministry, as Mark portrays it. Setting people free from the powers that oppress them, whether conceived of as personalized demons, as in Jesus' day, or as forces beyond their control, as in ours, was and is Jesus' agenda, according to Mark. It is to be part of bringing in God's reign, the kingdom of God, the "good news" of hope and liberation. Mark makes it very clear that the movement to bring hope and liberation is likely to encounter much opposition along the way, including from family and religious and political powers. It was and is important not to give up. Mark goes on directly to address this theme in what follows.

Reflection: How does Mark depict family power as an issue for Jesus and how do you see family power as a problem today?

Don't Give Up! (4:1–34)

Listening to Mark

^{4:1} And he started teaching again by the lake and a massive crowd flocked to him, so he got into a boat and sat in it on the lake while all the crowd was on land on the shore. ² And he was teaching them a lot using parables, and in his instruction he said to them, ³ "Listen. A sower went out to sow seed. ⁴ And while he was sowing, some seed fell beside the path and the birds came and ate it. ⁵ Others fell on stoney ground where there wasn't much soil, and it came up straightaway because there was no depth of soil ⁶ but when the sun came up, it was scorched and having no root, it dried up. ⁷ And others fell among thorns and the thorns came up and strangled it and it did not produce any grain. ⁸ And others fell on good soil and was productive, coming up and growing to end up producing a harvest, some a threefold yield, some a sixtyfold, and some a hundredfold." ⁹ And he added: "Whoever has ears, listen!"

¹⁰ And when he was on his own, those who were with him along with the twelve asked him about the parables ¹¹ and he told them, "The mystery of the kingdom of God is given to you, but for those outside everything comes in parables, ¹² so that seeing, they may not really see and have insight, and hearing, they may not really hear and have understanding, lest they turn and be forgiven."

¹³ Then he addresses them saying, "You don't get this parable? Then how will you get any of the parables? ¹⁴ The sower sows the word. ¹⁵ Those by the wayside where the seed was sown are the people who, when they hear, immediately Satan comes and removes the word sown into them. ¹⁶ Those sown on stoney ground are the people who, when they hear the word, immediately receive it with joy, ¹⁷ but have no root in themselves and are short lived and when persecution troubles hit them because of the word, immediately they stumble and fall. ¹⁸ And others sown among thorn bushes, these are people who hear the word ¹⁹ but worries about this life and the deceitfulness of wealth and greed

for other things come in and choke the word and they fail to produce a harvest. ²⁰ And those sown on good soil are those who hear the word, take it on board, and produce a harvest, some thirtyfold, some sixtyfold, some a hundredfold."

²¹ And he was telling them, "A lamp isn't something to put under a basket or under a bed, is it? Surely it is for putting on a lampstand. ²² For there is nothing hidden that will not be revealed nor anything secret that will not come to be known. ²³ If anyone has ears, listen!"

²⁴ And he told them, "Watch what you hear! With the measure you measure you will be measured and even more so. ²⁵ Whoever has, will be given more; and whoever doesn't have much, even what they have will be taken away from them."

²⁶ And he told them, "The kingdom of God is like when a man sows seed on his land ²⁷ and goes to sleep and gets up day after day and the seed sprouts and grows and he has no idea how. ²⁸ Of its own accord the earth produces fruit, first the blade then the ear and then the full head of grain on the ear. ²⁹ When the grain is ripe, he immediately sends in the sickle because it's harvest time."

³⁰ And he said, "What is the kingdom of God like and with what parable can I depict it? ³¹ It is like a mustard seed, which someone sows in the ground, tinier than all other seeds on earth, ³² and when it is sown, it comes up and becomes the largest shrub of all and produces such big branches, that the birds can rest under its shade."

³³ With many such parables he spoke his message to them as much as they could listen to. ³⁴ He did not address them except in parables, but in private he explained everything to his own disciples.

Thinking about Mark

Mark presents his story of Jesus in a way that has Jesus not only gaining wide popularity but also at the same time facing opposition and misunderstanding, including from his own family. He next makes use of a collection of parables about seeds. They will have been much loved and repeated over the decades and likely grouped together because of their common imagery of seeds and harvest.

Mark begins with the note that Jesus boarded a boat close to shore because of the thronging crowd, a strategy deployed already earlier according to Mark 3:9. Mark mentions that Jesus used parables and will comment about their role. The first parable is very simple and, for the audience in Galilee, the food bowl for Israel because of its wheat farms, very familiar. The pattern of sowing appears to have been to sow first and then plough in the seed. Yes, of course, some would fall on the path, some of rocky ground, some among thorns, but never mind: there would be a harvest.

The harvest Jesus projects is huge. The message is simple: don't give up! The message of the good news will bear fruit! Those who will have been listening to Mark's story thus far will have nodded their heads: plenty of opposition so far but look at the crowds! Don't let opposition get you down! Most of those listening to Mark would also have known how the story develops, or at least, how it ends: not just opposition, but crucifixion! But then, resurrection and new beginnings.

Jesus often told parables and most reflect everyday life, as though everyday life was also his Bible. They were a rich source for reflection, and this certainly appears to have been the case with this first parable of the sower sowing seed. Mark is about to bring an interpretation of the parable that had applied it to life in the church, but before that, he adds his own comments in 4:10–12. They appear to turn the purpose of parables as a form of communication on its head by saying they were told not to communicate the message but to block it! Insiders get the secret information; outsiders are blocked out. This may leave insiders feeling good, even smug, and perhaps that was intended.

A gentler interpretation is that parables function in a way that does not explain but opens up the possibility that people may see something new. A penny dropped experience, some would say. They are extended images. Some people will get the point and others will not. They will put two and two together, as it were. "I get it," they might say. The hope is that all will "get it." The aim is not to exclude, but to offer the possibility that people might twig to what is meant.

Mark then brings an interpretation of the parable that uses it not to enable sudden insight, but to explain opposition, or, more particularly, to explain why some people who joined the movement, the church and its message, then abandoned it (4:13–20). Seed sown on the path and snatched up by birds serves to illustrate those who hear the message and don't receive it. The other categories, however, are about people who do receive the message (and join the movement). The pressure of persecution (stoney ground) and the seduction of wealth (thorns) lead them to give up their faith. Only those who stick with it bear fruit.

The interpretation is both a challenge to hearers not to succumb to failure, but also a consolation to Jesus-followers aggrieved by those abandoning their faith by explaining why they do so. Mark reinforces the challenge by having Jesus state the obvious: you light a lamp? Let it shine (4:21)! Two more warnings follow: don't think you can hide the truth about yourself (4:22–23) and don't opt for half measures or you will lose what you have (4:24–25).

Mark then returns to another parable in the parable collection. A sower does not understand how it all works, from seed to harvest. He just scatters the seed, and the harvest happens (4:26–29). Our science means we can know much more, but even so, the message is the same: do it! Trust the process! The parable of the mustard seed (4:30–32) has a similarly positive message. Although it is a slight exaggeration to say a mustard seed is the smallest seed or that it grows into the greatest of all shrubs, the parable does illustrate the contrast between the small and the great—it is a tiny seed and it does grow into at least a big bush. The message is clear. Don't give up! Trust in hope!

The mention of birds sheltering under mustard shrubs may be more than just incidental. Biblical tradition is known to have used the image of birds to speak of foreign nations (Ezek 31:6). It is possible that Mark or the tradition before him intends a hint at the Jesus movement's reaching out to gentiles. The image of the nations, the gentiles, also coming to Jerusalem to worship at the temple and learn the ways of God (Isa 2:2–4; 25:6–7) is an inspiring vision that helped inform early Christian thought, from Paul's bringing the collection of offerings from the gentile churches to Jerusalem (1 Cor 16:1–4), to Matthew's image of the noblest of the gentiles, the magi, bringing gifts to the baby in Bethlehem (2:1–12). As we shall see, the message of gentiles' inclusion is an important theme later in Mark.

Mark rounds off his section on parables with another general remark, again suggesting that Jesus addressed the public in parables but gave explanations to his disciples (4:33–34), which may reflect more how Mark sees it than how it happened historically. On the other hand, Mark will go on to show that the disciples, for all their privileges, often lacked understanding.

Reflection: What lies behind the hope implied in these parables and how important is hope and having a basis for hope in our world today? What can be its basis?

Faith All at Sea (4:35–41)

Listening to Mark

⁴:³⁵ Then on that day as evening came, he said to them, "Let's go over to the other side." ³⁶ So leaving the crowd, they took him, already in the boat; and other boats were also sailing along with it. ³⁷ And a storm blew up and waves broke over the boat, so that it was already beginning to fill with water. ³⁸ He was in the stern asleep on a cushion and they wake him up and say, "Teacher, doesn't it matter to you that our lives are in danger?" ³⁹ And he got up, rebuked the wind and said to the sea, "Be still!" and it became still, and the wind dropped and there was a great calm. ⁴⁰ And he said to them, "Why are you afraid? Do you still not have faith?" ⁴¹ And they were overwhelmed with awe and said to one another, "Who is this that even the wind and sea obey him?"

Thinking about Mark

Mark follows what appears to be an optimistic assessment of the faith of the disciples with a decidedly negative one when he has Jesus declare: "Why are you afraid? Do you still not have faith?" (4:40). More rebukes will follow as the disciples fail to see what at least Mark thinks they (and his hearers) should see.

Winds could come up suddenly on the lake. I experienced that once personally on a boat trip from Tiberias on its western shore up to Capernaum on its northern shore. Probably a sea wind sweeping up the valley from the Mediterranean, the gusts set us rocking, as what had been a very calm crossing neared its end. One could well imagine that the turbulence might just as quickly subside.

Mark's story does not assume natural processes, which might satisfy our trained minds. He has received the story as a miracle. Jesus can change the weather, still the storm. He does so by giving it instructions and by expecting to be obeyed: "Peace be still!" Those who passed on the story knew why he did so. Their science told them that demons could control wind and storm, so that Jesus was again showing that by the Spirit he could not only cast out demons but force them to obey him. The disciples needed to believe that he could do so.

For those listening to the story with knowledge of Israel's faith tradition, the story will have evoked memories of stories they had heard before, such as the story of Jonah asleep in the boat and then turfed overboard and the Psalms that acclaim God's ability to calm the waves (65:10; 89:9). God's Spirit, therefore, could do the same through Jesus.

Mark will bring another such story when he reports Jesus' walking on water, to whose symbolic significance we return below (6:47-52). Unlike Jesus' exorcisms, his casting out of demons, a task he also commissions his disciples to fulfill, these nature miracles appear not to belong to the disciples' repertoire. Knowing the devastating effects of floods and tragedies at sea, how could we not want the disciples and us as their successors to be able to offer such help?

Like the quasi-magical multiplication of the loaves to feed thousands, a gift we would, of course, also dearly love to employ in response to the desperately poor and hungry, these stories have, in that sense, no continuing relevance, at least as far as human need is concerned. Their function was primarily to win followers. They served, we might say, propaganda, and challenge our credulity.

They also had the potential to distract from Jesus' message. In a number of New Testament writings, we see traces of discomfit with using signs and wonders to attract a following. John's Gospel is quite direct when it reports Jesus' response to those who believed in him because of the wonders he performed, stating that he did not believe in them (2:23-25)! It then has Nicodemus say he believed Jesus came from God because of the miracles, only to be told by Jesus that he needed to start again, to be born again, because such a faith misses the point (3:1-3). Similarly, Matthew's Sermon on the Mount has Jesus disown followers whose faith was based on wonders (7:21-23) and who neglect its real meaning; and Paul confronts such faith with his famous chapter on love (1 Corinthians 13).

One might see Mark's use of the story to expose the disciples' faith as all at sea, as moving beyond the miracle, but Mark surely would not have doubted that Jesus did such things and those writers who seek to shift the focus from the wonder to deeper meaning were not thereby expressing any skepticism of the kind that modern readers regularly bring to such stories.

Jesus scolds them, indeed, because they failed to trust that he could control the weather. Such stories belong to Mark's world and reflect its science of natural phenomena as controlled by demons, a very different world from ours. Part of our respect for the New Testament and its authors is the acknowledgment of such differences and not to pretend otherwise. There is more than enough that we do share with them.

Reflection: Why does Mark assume Jesus could change the weather and how do we deal with the gulf between our understanding of meteorology and theirs?

2

The Expansion

Israel and Beyond (5:1–43)

Listening to Mark

^{5:1} They went over the other side of the lake to the region of the Gerasenes. ² And as they were disembarking from the boat suddenly a man with an unclean spirit came out from among the tombs and confronted him. ³ He was living in the cemetery, and so far no one had been able to restrain him, not even with chains ⁴ because often he had been bound with shackles but the chains and shackles had been wrenched open by him and no one could tame him. ⁵ And there he was, day and night among the tombs and up in the hills shouting out and cutting himself with stones. ⁶ Seeing Jesus from a distance, he ran over to him and fell down before him, ⁷ shouting with a loud voice, "What do you want with me, Jesus, Son of the Most High God? In God's name I implore you, don't torment me!" ⁸ He said to him, "Unclean spirit get out of the man!" ⁹ and asked him, "What's your name?" He replied, "Legion's my name and there's lots of us." ¹⁰ And he kept insisting that he not send them out of the area. ¹¹ Now there was a large herd of pigs grazing on the hillside. ¹² And so they implored him, "Send us to the pigs so we can get inside them." ¹³ He gave them permission and the unclean spirits went off and entered the pigs and the herd then charged down the bank into the lake, around two thousand of them, and they drowned in the lake.

¹⁴ Now the pig farmers fled and told people in the town and the region, so they came out to see what had happened. ¹⁵ And they approached Jesus and saw the man who had been demon possessed, the one who had the legion, sitting down fully clothed and now making sense, and they were scared. ¹⁶ And those who had seen how it all happened, including what happened to the pigs, reported what took place. ¹⁷ They then started urging him to leave their territory.

¹⁸ When they were getting back into the boat, the man who had been demon possessed asked him if he could come with him, ¹⁹ but he didn't permit him to do so, but instead told him, "Go home to your people and tell them what the Lord has done for you and how he had mercy on you." ²⁰ And he went off and started to proclaim in the Decapolis region what Jesus had done for him and everyone was amazed.

²¹ Then Jesus crossed over by boat to the other side and a large crowd gathered to meet him; and he was by the lakeside. ²² And one of the senior synagogue leaders, called Jairus, saw him and fell at his feet, ²³ pleading with him over and over again, saying, "My daughter is at the point of death; please come and lay hands on her to heal her so that she'll survive." ²⁴ And he went off with him and a big crowd followed him and thronged him.

²⁵ And there was a woman who had experienced irregular bleeding for twelve years ²⁶ who had suffered a lot at the hands of doctors and had spent all her money to no benefit but rather things were just getting worse. ²⁷ Having heard about Jesus, she approached in the crowd and touched his garment from behind, ²⁸ because she was saying, if only I can touch his clothes, I will be made well. ²⁹ And immediately the source of the bleeding stopped, and she knew in her body that she had been healed of her affliction. ³⁰ However, straightaway Jesus sensed in himself that power had gone out from him, so turning around to the crowd, he said, "Who touched my clothes?" ³¹ And his disciples said, "Don't you see the crowd pressing in on you and are you really saying, 'Who touched me?'" ³² So he was looking around to see who had done so ³³ when the women, feeling very afraid and trembling and knowing what had happened to her, came and fell at his feet and told him the whole truth. ³⁴ He then said to her, "Daughter, your faith has made you well. Go in peace and be healed of your affliction."

35 While he was still speaking, people came from the synagogue leader's place saying, "Your daughter has died. Why keep hassling the teacher?" 36 Jesus picked up what they were saying and so says to the synagogue leader, "Don't worry. Just have faith!" 37 And he did not permit anyone to accompany him except Peter and James and John, James' brother. 38 They go into the synagogue leader's house and see a commotion with people weeping and a lot of wailing. 39 Going inside, he says to them, "Why are you so upset and weeping? The child hasn't died but is just sleeping." 40 They laughed at him. Then he tells them all to get outside and takes the father of the child and her mother and those close to them and goes in to where the child was. 41 Taking the child by the hand, he says, "*Talitha cum*!," which means "Young girl, get up!" 42 And straightaway the girl got up and started walking around. She was twelve years old. And they were really astounded. 43 And he pressed on them strictly not to make this known and told them that she should be given something to eat.

Thinking about Mark

Mark next takes us beyond the land of Israel across the Jordan to Gerasa, about 60 km from Lake Galilee (5:1–20). It is the first episode where Jesus reaches into the world of the gentiles and a significant pointer forward to Mark's own day when the gospel had been reaching wide into the Roman Empire. Mark places this episode in his storyline directly beside the story of the healing of the girl and the woman, in the land of Israel, emphasized symbolically by giving the age of the girl as twelve and identifying the woman's plight as having last twelve years, twelve being a symbol of Israel and its twelve tribes (5:21–43). The two panels—Gerasa in gentile land and the women in Israel—symbolize that the offer of the gospel is not only to Israel but also beyond Israel to the nations.

Cultural assumptions had shaped how the stories had been told. From a traditional Jewish perspective Jesus was entering territory where Jews might encounter the ritually unclean. That applied to being in a gentile land but especially to encountering a man who lived among tombs. The reference to the herd of pigs nearby, unclean animals, further reinforces the alien context.

Even more striking is Mark's depiction of the man as demon possessed, wild and uncontrolled, the human equivalent of a raging storm. His words, shouted at Jesus, "What do you want with me, Jesus, Son of the Most High God? In God's name I implore you, don't torment me!" (5:7) recall those of the unclean spirits in the opening episode of Jesus' public ministry: "What have you got to do with us, Jesus of Nazareth? Have you come to destroy us? I know who you are, the Holy One of God" (1:24). The assumption was that demons who belong in the spirit world know who Jesus is. Mark's hearers will realize that what the demons know, they as listeners have heard in the voice from heaven at Jesus' baptism (1:11). The fear expressed by the demons that Jesus might destroy or torment them reflects the belief that Jesus is to fulfill the role of Messiah/Son of Man judge at the end of time.

In the dialogue that follows, the demons in the man call themselves "legion," a term for a major division in the Roman army. We might speculate that the story reflects the fact that Rome's forces had reached the region and also that they were seen as demonic or in league with the demonic world. Jesus negotiates with the demons and agrees to expel them into a herd of around two thousand pigs, who then rush off down a cliff and drown in the lake. The story may reflect the fact that the legion's standard bore the image of a pig. Descent into the sea reflects the belief that the depths of the sea, the abyss, is the home of demons. The story is slightly bizarre because to reach the Sea of Galilee, where they are assumed to have drowned, the pigs would have had to embark on a thirty-seven-mile (sixty-kilometer) journey! Symbolic embellishment of such stories sometimes results in such anomalies. Matthew relieves it only somewhat by having the event take place near Gadara, only about five or six miles (nine to ten kilometers) away from the Sea (8:28).

The sequel to the exorcism was initially hostility on the part of the pig farmers—understandably—but then we hear a conversation between Jesus and the liberated man, where Jesus told him to go home and tell his story. The man became then one of the many followers who did not literally follow, but stayed where they were and spread the good news of what they had found. He serves as a model.

The story bristles with assumptions about uncleanness, which will have been significant for Jewish hearers of the story in its early retellings. Mark shows no concern to address such issues; nor does he report any action on Jesus' part to purify himself when returning to the land of Israel, as would have been required, but focuses instead on Jesus as the liberator

THE EXPANSION

who can set people free from their demons and on the significance of Jesus' reaching out to the gentile world.

He moves directly on to showing Jesus active on the western side of the lake, in Israel, his second panel of his two-panel portrait, which celebrates the gospel coming to both Jews and gentiles (5:21–43). Mark again employs the sandwich technique of composition as he had done, for instance in 3:21–35, in depicting Jesus' family's response. The story is located right at the heart of Jewish faith as it portrays a synagogue leader, Jairus, seeking help for his daughter who was facing death.

Mentioning Jesus' response and his setting off for the man's home (5:21–24), Mark interrupts the story by referring to a woman they met along the way (5:52–34). Mark describes her plight as that of having abnormal vaginal bleeding; and now she is at her wits end, having exhausted all attempts to get medical help and finding her situation getting worse. Jewish hearers would have been aware that this also put her in a state of uncleanness (Lev 15:25–27; cf. 15:19–24), which required her to isolate socially. She hoped that by touching Jesus' garment—something she should, therefore, not have done—she would be healed. Mark ignores the purity issue, as he had ignored the purity issues in the previous story. His focus is on the divine power and so he tells us that when she touched his garment, she was immediately healed. We find belief in such quasi-magical healing influence through touching clothes also in 6:56.

Mark assumes such healing is possible and that the healer would sense such healing power being transmitted, and so has Jesus ask who touched him. Mark depicts the disciples as out of touch with what had happened when they observe very reasonably that, surrounded by people, any number of people might have touched Jesus. They needed to believe that Jesus had special powers. The woman confesses and Jesus reassures her: "Daughter, your faith has made you well; go in peace, and be healed of your disease" (5:34).

Mark returns to the story of Jairus' daughter (5:35–43). She had died in the meantime and lamentation had begun. Mark has Jesus defy their grieving and their ridicule at his suggestion she was just sleeping, bring Peter, James, and John, the three leading disciples, with him, take the girl's hand, and raise her back to life. Mark reports Jesus' original words in Aramaic: "Talitha cum," which he explains, means "Little girl, get up!" Some, hearing the story, may have heard these as magical words, typically expressed in a foreign language as sometimes by such healers, but that does not appear to be Mark's intent. Mark also gives no attention to the fact that

Jesus, by entering the house where there was a corpse, let alone touching it, would have been rendered unclean (Num 19:11–22).

Mark clearly understands Jesus' act as a resuscitation. The girl had, indeed, died. Jesus brought her back to life. Only God could do such things. Jesus could do so by God's Spirit. Adding the note that she was twelve years of age, like the reference to women's plight going on for twelve years, reminds readers that these are people of Israel, the nation of the twelve tribes. Thus, panel one in Mark 5 celebrated outreach to gentiles; panel two celebrates outreach to Israel.

Stories can have multiple functions. Mark may well intend that his hearers sense a connection between the two women, not only through the numerics of twelve, but also through the gynecological link. One has abnormal vaginal bleeding, the other is of an age where normal menstruation might begin. Beyond that, it would also remind hearers that the gospel reaches not only to both Jew and gentile; it also reaches out to embrace both female and male.

Mark's primary focus appears to have been to highlight Jesus' power and his reaching out to both Israel and the gentile world. In our cross-cultural engagement with Mark, some of Mark's assumptions, such as demonology, therapeutic impact mediated through touching garments, and resuscitation on command are far from assumptions that we can share. Others, such as the inclusivity of Jew and gentile, female and male, we can embrace. Mark, himself, appears no longer to share assumptions that informed these stories, including about the uncleanness of the gentile world, which in 7:1–23 he will, in any case, have Jesus set aside, and possibly also assumptions about transmitted impurity through touch of a menstruant or equivalent or of a corpse. Such contrary assumptions not only explain Mark's failure to address such issues but would have also been significant in affirming openness and acceptance where formerly there were barriers.

Reflection: What are some of the Jewish cultural assumptions lying behind these stories and where does Mark put the emphasis? How can we embrace and apply Mark's emphasis in our world?

THE EXPANSION

Confronting Rejection (6:1–29)

Listening to Mark

⁶:¹ He then went on from there and came to his hometown with his disciples following him. ² When the Sabbath came, he started teaching in the synagogue and many who heard him were astonished, saying, "Where did this fellow get all this? What is this wisdom he's been given and how come such miracles are occurring by his hands? ³ Isn't this the builder's boy, Mary's son, and isn't he James and Joses and Jude and Simon's brother?" And they started to take offence at him. ⁴ Jesus said to them, "A prophet is not without honor except in his hometown, and among his kin and in his family home." ⁵ And he couldn't do any miracles there, except for laying his hands on a few sick people and healing them. ⁶ And he marveled at their lack of faith. So he set off teaching in the towns around about.

⁷ He also summoned the twelve and started sending them out in pairs, giving them authority over unclean spirits. ⁸ And he told them not to take anything with them on the road, but only a staff, but no food, no purse, and no money in their belt, ⁹ but just go, wearing sandals and not to put on two overgarments. ¹⁰ And he told them, "When you enter someone's house, stay there until you leave. ¹¹ And whatever place does not welcome you or want to hear you, leave them and shake the dust off your feet as evidence against them." ¹² And they went out proclaiming that people should repent ¹³ and they were expelling demons and were anointing many sick people with oil and healing them.

¹⁴ King Herod heard about him because he was getting quite a name and people were saying John the Baptizer had been raised back to life from the dead and that's how come the miracles are being done by him. Others were saying he was Elijah. ¹⁵ And again others, that he was the prophet or one of the prophets. ¹⁶ When Herod heard this, he was saying, "John whom I decapitated, it's him, risen from the dead." ¹⁷ For Herod had sent and arrested John and bound him in prison because of Herodias, Philip, his brother's wife, because he had married her. ¹⁸ For

John was telling Herod, "It is unlawful for you to take your brother's wife." ¹⁹ Herodias resented him and wanted to have him dead, but had not succeeded, ²⁰ because Herod feared John, knowing that he was a good and holy man, and so retained him in prison. He found him perplexing when he listened to him but was very happy to hear him.

²¹ Then an opportune time afforded itself when Herod put on a party for his birthday, inviting nobles and commanders and leading people in Galilee. ²² And when his stepdaughter, Herodias, came in and danced, she charmed Herod and those reclining around him and so he said to the girl, "Ask me whatever you like and I'll give it to you." ²³ And he insisted with an oath saying, "I'll give you whatever you like up to half my kingdom." ²⁴ And she went straight out to her mother and asked her, "What shall I ask for?" And she said, "The head of John the Baptist." ²⁵ She immediately hurried back to the king and said, "I want you to give me at once the head of John the Baptist on a platter." ²⁶ The king was deeply troubled because he had sworn an oath and because of those present, so was unwilling to turn her down. ²⁷ So immediately the king sent off his executioner with the instruction to bring his head, who then went off and decapitated him in the prison ²⁸ and brought his head on a platter and gave it to the girl who then gave it to her mother. ²⁹ When his disciples heard about it, they came and retrieved his corpse and laid it in a tomb.

Thinking about Mark

In his storyline of Jesus' life Mark brings us to Nazareth where Jesus grew up. He had already referred to Jesus' family in 3:20–21, 30–35, in the context of rejection. Now the focus is the response he received from his hometown synagogue. He clearly had freedom to teach there, as he had in synagogues in the region. The locals had known him and are surprised at his apparent wisdom and achievements.

Mark invites us to imagine the scene and their saying: "How can someone just like us turn out like this? He's just the boy from down the road, Mary's son, who became a carpenter. We all know the family; they're all here with us: James, Joses, Judas, Simon, and his sisters." As Mark put it, "And they started to take offence at him" (6:3).

THE EXPANSION

It will not have been the first time for a high achiever to encounter such a response and will not have been the last. Some call it "the tall poppy syndrome": cut it down to size! Jesus cites how prophets had also faced it: "A prophet is not without honor except in his hometown, and among his kin and in his family home" (6:4). They faced it even in their own families, in their own home. When Matthew and Luke rewrite this story, they omit the reference to one's own house, as they also omitted reference in chapter 3 to Jesus' family wanting to restrain him fearing he was mad, for they begin their stories with angels making very clear to Mary and Joseph that the opposite would be true.

Mark bemoans the fact that the locals' negative response limited Jesus' opportunity to heal to just a few people. Mark then has Jesus move on, teaching in surrounding villages, and setting up a strategy for expanding hope and healing. His disciples had accompanied him to Nazareth. Mark tells us how Jesus sent them out in pairs, probably for security (6:7). He describes their role as doing what Jesus had been doing, namely, calling people to repent and turn to God, expelling demons, and performing acts of healing, including a reference to one of the means of healing: anointing people with oil.

Beyond identifying their task, Mark has Jesus give very specific instructions about their lifestyle (6:8–11). They are to be almost like beggars, at least to the extent that they were to be dependent on others for their survival, much as this had also been the case when they were traveling with Jesus. They were to expect to be hosted by sympathetic locals for food and accommodation and not to hassle if this hospitality was not forthcoming, but to let rejection be, shaking off the dust from their feet. Mark may mean more than that when he has Jesus indicate that the symbolic act of shaking the dust from their feet would indicate judgment. Apart from that, they could take a staff (probably for protection against wild animals) but "no food, no purse and no money in their belt, but just go, wearing sandals and not to put on two overgarments" (6:8–9).

In a deeply impoverished society this approach would not have worked, but it did work in Galilee because, despite significant levels of poverty, some did have the means to offer support. Matthew and Luke apparently knew a second source for these instructions beside Mark. Luke then includes both, repeating Mark's version of the sending of the twelve and then adding a second account, which he now symbolically describes as the sending out of seventy (9:1–6; 10:1–12). Matthew, by contrast, merges the two accounts into the one sending of the twelve but retains the even stricter version of the second source forbidding even the taking of a staff (10:1–15).

Matthew and Luke bring us also some further instructions that would have applied originally to such strategies. "Do not worry about your life, what you will eat or what you will drink, or about your body, what you will wear," appealing to how in nature God feeds the birds and clothes the grass of the field, and how lilies grow (Matt 6:25–34; Luke 12:22–32). Paul reaped criticism for being pragmatic and deciding that a more caring option for him in some circumstances was not to live in such dependence on others but to work part time to support his ministry (1 Corinthians 9).

One might wonder how people in Mark's time, hearing his gospel read, would view such instructions. We can imagine that they would continue to see the church's agenda as teaching and bringing healing, including through exorcism, and may well have been providing support for their preachers and teachers. Most of Mark's hearers would not have been itinerants, but locals. Financial support for people given special tasks was and remains essential, though we may imagine that in Mark's time Paul's commonsense approach would have prevailed: What makes best sense in terms of what is the most effective way forward in response to human need? Love loosens rules and ordinances to ensure flexibility and effectiveness.

Rejection, the theme at Nazareth, and touched on briefly in the commissioning of disciples, returns dramatically in what follows, for Mark now tells the story of John the Baptist's fate (6:14–29). The underlying thought is that such a fate will also await Jesus. This sense is already implied in Mark's comments that Herod Antipas, who had executed John, feared he might have returned. We are probably to assume that Mark suggests that Antipas could believe that the spirit of one person might return in another. Mark mentions what others were thinking: the return of Elijah's spirit or of one of the prophets. Mark will return to such views among the populace where Jesus' identity is again in focus (8:27–28).

Herod Antipas was the son of Herod the Great, who had ruled a swathe of territory, including Judea and Galilee, from 37–34 BCE. On Herod the Great's death, his territory was divided among his sons, Archelaus taking Judea, Samaria, and Idumea; Philip, the Golan Heights and adjacent area; and Antipas, Galilee and Perea. Herod Antipas was not, in fact a king, but a tetrarch, a regional ruler of less status than a king.

Herod the Great had a number of wives and as a result his children were a mixture of siblings and stepsiblings. One of Antipas' stepbrothers was the one whom Mark calls Herod Philip, different from the Philip just mentioned, and otherwise simply called Herod. This Herod was the son of Herod the Great and the daughter of the high priest, Simon, and was married to his niece, Herodias, also niece of Antipas. Marrying nephews was forbidden in biblical law (Lev 18:12–14), but not marrying nieces. The Sadducees and the Essenes took a very strict view claiming that prohibiting nephew marriages must imply forbidding niece marriages, even if it is not explicitly stated. The Pharisees rejected this view. Mark does not indicate that it was a problem for Antipas to marry a woman who was his niece.

The problem, Mark suggests, which brought John the Baptist's criticism, was that he married his sister-in-law, his stepbrother's divorced wife, Herodias (6:18). This was not a case of bigamy, because she had divorced her husband, Herod Philip. Marrying the divorced wife of one's stepbrother is something perfectly acceptable in many legislatures today, but not on John's (and Mark's) reading of Lev 18:16, which forbids marrying one's sister-in-law.

Josephus, the Jewish historian, writing in the late first century CE tells us more. Antipas had stayed with Herod Philip, his stepbrother, on some occasions and developed a relationship with Herod's wife, Herodias, that eventually led to the divorce and to Antipas and Herodias getting together. One might imagine that this behavior would have been seen as unacceptable, but Mark does not mention it. The new relationship also entailed Antipas divorcing his then-current wife, the daughter of King Aretas of the Nabatean kingdom. As Josephus tells us, Aretas would later confront Antipas in battle in part because of this, defeating him, and having him deposed.

Might the divorces have influenced John the Baptist's attitude? Mark does not say so. We might even speculate that the situation put divorce on Jesus' agenda and had him court questions about divorce, as reported in Mark 10, but on this, too, Mark is silent. We are left with a single extremely strict criticism, with which we can probably assume that Jesus was in agreement. The broader historical context suggests that Antipas would have seen such a popular leader as John as dangerous and a potential cause of trouble and would have executed him primarily on those grounds, just as Pilate would deal with Jesus as potentially subversive.

Mark appears to have inherited a popular bizarre tale about John's fate, replete with dramatic detail. In a flashback to tell of John's demise, Mark tells us about Antipas' birthday party (6:21–29). The men were together celebrating and being entertained, and, reflecting the normal pattern for such male occasions, the women—or at least the respectable women, like wives and family—were located elsewhere, adjacent to the main gathering where the men were on their own, with entertainers. Herodias' daughter, Salome, as Josephus names her (in contrast to Mark, who calls her Herodias, like her mother), contributed to the entertainment by dancing before the men. We may assume she was by this time a teenager and the rest is left to our imagination: "she charmed Herod and those reclining around him" (6:22). Was this voluntary or exploitation or abuse? Mark gives no indication. His story tells us that Antipas falls for her and promises, "I'll give you whatever you like up to half my kingdom" (6:23). Besotted? Drunk? She goes out to where her mother, Herodias, is with the respectable women and returns wanting John the Baptist's head. Such was the grotesque outcome.

Beyond the tale, however fanciful it might have been, is the somber reality that Antipas executed John and Pilate would execute Jesus. John's disciples, Mark tells, retrieved his body and buried him in a tomb (6:29). Mark may thereby be informing us incidentally that John's movement continued, something we see reflected some decades later in John's Gospel. John's fate foreshadows Jesus' fate. Rejection hovers.

Reflection: What were the patterns of exercising discipleship and ministry in the time of Jesus and the time of the early church and what relevance or equivalence do they have today? Who are the Herod Antipas figures in the world today?

THE EXPANSION

Abounding (6:30–56)

Listening to Mark

6:30 Then the apostles come back to Jesus and tell him all they had done and taught and **31** he says to them, "Come on away to an isolated place by yourselves and rest up a bit." For many were coming and going and they scarcely had opportunity to eat. **32** So they set off by boat to an isolated spot where they could be on their own, **33** but some saw them departing and recognized them and set off on foot from all the towns to reach there and got there ahead of them. **34** Seeing the large crowd, Jesus was moved with compassion for them, because they were like sheep without a shepherd and he started doing lots of teaching.

35 When it was already quite late, his disciples approached him and said, "This is an isolated spot and it's already very late. **36** Send them off into the towns and hamlets in the vicinity to go and buy something to eat." **37** But he replied, "You give them something to eat." They responded, "You mean we are to and spend two hundred denarii buying food to give them to eat?" **38** He replied, "How much bread do you have? Go and see!" They found out and said, "Five loaves and two fish."

39 Then he instructed them to set everyone out on the green grass in groups. **40** And they sat down in groups of hundreds and fifties. **41** And taking the five loaves and the two fish, looking up to heaven, he blessed them and broke them up and distributed them to the disciples for them to hand them out and he divided the fish up for everyone. **42** And they all ate and were satisfied, **43** and they gathered the leftovers of the bread and fish into twelve baskets. **44** Those who had eaten numbered five thousand men.

45 He straightaway got his disciples to embark on the boat and sail off to the other side, to Bethsaida, while he dismissed the crowd. **46** And then taking his leave of them, he went off up a mountain to pray. **47** And in the evening the boat was on the lake and he was on his own on land. **48** But seeing them hard up against it in trying to make headway, because they were sailing into the wind, and it was the fourth watch of the night, he comes to them walking on the lake and intended to walk past them. ⁴⁹ But they saw him walking on the lake and thought it was a ghost and called out. ⁵⁰ For they all saw him and were scared. He straightaway spoke to them and said, "Cheer up. It's me. Don't be scared!" ⁵¹ And he got into the boat with them and the wind dropped and they were very amazed. ⁵² For they had not understood about the bread but had hardened hearts.

⁵³ Reaching land at Gennesaret, they went ashore. ⁵⁴ And as they were disembarking from the boat, some immediately recognized him ⁵⁵ and ran around the whole countryside and started bringing their sick people on stretchers to where he was. ⁵⁶ And wherever he entered hamlets or towns or country areas, they put the sick in the marketplaces and asked if they could touch the hem of his garment and as many as touched it were healed.

Thinking about Mark

Having looked back to report what had happened to John the Baptist, Mark returns to where he was in his storyline. He had reported Jesus' sending out his disciples in pairs (6:7) and now they return telling him of their exploits (6:30). Mark makes no mention of their reports in detail, but instead uses their return as a transition to the story of the feeding of the huge crowd of five thousand men (6:30-44).

Having the disciples come aside to rest for a while away from the crowds echoes what Jesus, himself, had done when first setting out on his mission (1:35). It models a pattern of self-care, but, unlike when he did it, there is no one to urge on them that they should not rest but respond to all the people wanting help. Mark mentioned also earlier that Jesus found himself in the crush of the crowds unable to eat (3:20) as here (6:31).

The intent and strategy of withdrawal made and makes sense, but what do you do when it does not work? Mark tells us that people saw them go and went after them, arriving ahead of them, so that their break was at most the time together in the boat. Confronted by such a big crowd so far from their homes and with the day becoming late Mark tells us that Jesus, who had engaged them with teaching, was filled with compassion (6:34). The explanation, because they were like "sheep without a shepherd," is an echo of the image of Israel in its need (Num 27:17; 2 Chr 18:16).

THE EXPANSION

In depicting the conversation between Jesus and his disciples, the latter are close to rude in protesting that there is no way they can feed such a crowd (6:35–37). This fits with Mark's tendency not to paint the disciples in the best of light. Mark shows Jesus taking control, setting the crowd out in groups of hundreds and fifties, and taking the five loaves and two fishes and miraculously making them sufficient to feed everyone.

The words, "he looked up to heaven, and blessed and broke the loaves, and gave them to his disciples to set before the people" (6:41) may well have evoked for some of Mark's hearers memory of Jesus' last meal, the inauguration of what became Holy Communion.

More directly significant in a symbolic sense are details such as setting the crowd out in fifties and hundreds, as in the wilderness, and the numbers twelve, five thousand, and possibly also five and two. These are symbols of Israel, like "sheep without a shepherd." Twelve is symbolic of Israel and its twelve tribes; five thousand may reflect the five books of the Law of Moses, Genesis to Deuteronomy, and possibly the number five does the same, and with two perhaps suggesting the two other main sections of the Old Testament, the Prophets and the Writings. There is, at the very least, a clear indication that Mark wants us to see the feeding of the five thousand as representing the feeding of Israel with the message of the gospel.

When we turn to Mark's account of the feeding of the four thousand, which takes place in gentile territory (8:1–10), we shall also find such use of symbolism and symbolic numbers. In 8:19–21 Mark has Jesus draw the attention of his disciples (and so of his hearers) to the significance of at least the numbers of baskets, twelve and seven. This helps us to appreciate that Mark means us to see the feeding of the five thousand as symbolic of the gospel coming to Israel and the four thousand as symbolic of the gospel coming to the gentiles. In both, there is an echo of the story of Israel's being fed by manna in the wilderness. However, Mark does not make this explicit, as the author of the Fourth Gospel does when he makes it part of the elaborate exchange he develops that has Jesus not only allude to the manna but assert that he alone is the true bread from heaven (John 6).

Matthew changes the focus from the symbolism of Israel and the gentiles to the wonder of the miracle itself and he changes both feedings to be of Jews, perhaps because he has Jesus instruct his disciples not to reach out to gentiles (10:5), something he would instruct them to do only after his resurrection (28:18–20). To Mark's count of "five thousand men" Matthew adds "beside women and children" (14:21), enhancing the miracle! Luke retains only the feeding of the five thousand, omitting the feeding of the four thousand and the material preceding it which offers the rationale for the expansion. For he, too, will have the outreach to gentiles ratified only after Peter's vision in Acts, which provides its rationale (Acts 10).

There is probably a symbolic intent also in the fantastic story that follows the feeding of the five thousand in Mark, namely the walking on the sea (6:47–52). Many of those listening to Mark's Gospel would sense that Jesus' walking over the waves symbolized his superiority over the evil spirits that had their abode in the deep. Mark had already reported that Jesus had sent the evil spirits in Gerasa careering in pigs back into the deep. When Jesus entered the boat, the wind abated, thus a second stilling of a storm after the first related in Mark 4. Mark often brings stories in pairs.

Mark's likely symbolic use of the story fits his understanding of hope and healing as being able to liberate people from evil spirits. At the same time, there is little doubt that Mark would have taken the story literally as evidence of Jesus' miraculous powers, which again the disciples failed to acknowledge, even if it is equally likely that he would not have assumed that future disciples would inherit such capacity and so be able to perform sea rescues. Matthew expands the story to have Peter invited to join Jesus on the water, Matthew's symbolic invention highlighting Peter's status but also his fallibility (14:22–33).

What Mark understands as the agenda of Jesus comes to the fore in yet another summary in the closing section, 6:53–56, recalling the summaries in 3:7–12 and 1:32–33. The reference to some seeking healing by touching Jesus' garment recalls the initiative of the woman with the hemorrhage in 5:28.

Reflection: How does Mark employ the stories of the mass feedings and what does their symbolism say? In what way can they function as symbols for us today?

THE EXPANSION

Overcoming Barriers (7:1—8:26)

Listening to Mark

7:1 The Pharisees approached him along with some of the scribes who had come up from Jerusalem, **2** and they saw some of his disciples eating food with unclean hands, that is, not ritually cleansed. **3** It mattered because the Pharisees and all Jews don't eat if they haven't purified their hands up to their wrists, in keeping with the tradition of the elders. **4** Similarly, when they come back from the marketplace, they do not eat unless they have ritually immersed themselves, and they observe many other such provisions, such as ritual washing of cups, pots, and bronze vessels. **5** So the Pharisees and the scribes asked him, "Why don't your disciples behave in keeping with the tradition of the elders, but instead eat food with defiled hands?"

6 Jesus responded, "Well did Isaiah prophesy about you hypocrites, as it is written, 'This people honors me with their lips, but their heart is far from me; **7** they worship me in vain, giving as their teaching the rules of human beings.' **8** You abandon God's commandment and hold instead to the tradition created by human beings." **9** And he went on, "You sure do abandon God's commandment in order to stick to your tradition. **10** For Moses said, 'Honor your father and mother' and 'Anyone speaking against father or mother, let them be put to death.' **11** But you say that if a person declares to father or mother 'the assistance I am obliged to offer you is *corban*,' that is, a sacred offering, **12** you exempt them from doing anything for their father or mother. **13** You thereby render the word of God void in the interests of the tradition you have received, and you do many things like that."

14 Then summoning the crowd again, he declared, "Listen, all of you and understand this: **15** nothing entering a person from outside them can render a person ritually unclean, but it's what comes out of people that makes them dirty." **17** And when he left the crowd and went inside the house, his disciples asked him about this parable, **18** and he answered, "Are you lacking in understanding, too? Don't you see that everything from outside that enters a person cannot render them unclean, ¹⁹ because it doesn't enter their mind but their stomach and then exits into the toilet." In this way he was declaring all foods clean as such. ²⁰ Then he went on to say, "What comes out of people, that's what renders people defiled. ²¹ For from people's minds come evil thoughts, sexual immorality, theft, murder, ²² adultery, greed, deceit, lust, envy, slander, pride, and stupidity, ²³ and these are what defile people."

²⁴ Setting off from there, he went to the region of Tyre. He went inside a house and did not want anyone to know he was there, but there was no escape ²⁵ because straightaway a woman who had heard about him, whose daughter had an unclean spirit, came and fell at his feet. ²⁶ The woman was a gentile, a Syrophoenician by birth. She was asking him to expel the demon from her daughter. ²⁷ His response was, "Let the children be fed first. It is not right to take the children's food and throw it to the dogs." ²⁸ But she countered, "Master, the dogs get to eat the children's crumbs from under the table." ²⁹ He replied, "For saying this, go. The demon has left your daughter." ³⁰ When she got home to her house, the child was lying on her bed and the demon had left her.

³¹ Then he left the region of Tyre and Sidon again for the Sea of Galilee and went over to the Decapolis region. ³² And people brought a deaf man with a speech impediment to him and asked him to lay his hand on him. ³³ And taking him aside from the crowd on his own, he put his fingers into his ears and with spittle on his fingers touched his tongue. ³⁴ Then looking up to heaven with a sigh, he said, "*Ephphatha*!"—which means "Be opened!" ³⁵ And straightaway his ears were opened and what bound his tongue was released and he started talking normally. ³⁶ And he gave them instructions that they should not tell anyone. ³⁷ But the more he told them not to, the more they spread the news. And they were really amazed, declaring that he had done that so well and was enabling deaf people to hear and those without a voice to speak.

⁸:¹ Those days it happened again that there was a large crowd who did not have anything to eat. So, summoning the disciples, he said to them. ² "I have compassion on the crowd, because they have been with me now for three days and they don't have anything to eat. ³ And if I send them off home hungry, they'll faint on the way and some of them come from a long way away." ⁴ His disciples replied, "Where can anyone get anything to feed them with here in the outback?"⁵ So he asked them, "How many loaves do you have?" And they said, "Seven."

⁶ So he told the crowd to sit down on the ground. And taking the seven loaves he gave thanks and broke them up into pieces and gave them to his disciples to distribute and they distributed them to the crowd. ⁷ And they had a few fish and having blessed them, he told them to distribute them, too. ⁸ They ate and were sated, and they picked up the pieces, seven baskets full. ⁹ There were around four thousand people. And then he sent them off.

¹⁰ Then, getting into the boat with his disciples, he came to the region of Dalmanutha. ¹¹ The Pharisees came out to him and started insisting that he give them a sign from heaven, putting him to the test. ¹² But he sighed in his spirit and says to them, "Why is this generation wanting a sign? Truly I tell you, no way will a sign be given this generation!" ¹³ And leaving them, he again embarked and sailed off to the other side. ¹⁴ Now they forgot to take any food except for one loaf they had with them in the boat. ¹⁵ And he warned them, "Beware of the yeast of the Pharisees and the yeast of Herod." ¹⁶ But they began to discuss among themselves whether this was because they had no bread. ¹⁷ Picking this up, he said, "Why are you talking about not having bread? Don't you yet realize and get the point? Do you have closed minds? ¹⁸ As they say, 'with eyes but not looking, with ears but not hearing'? Don't you remember, ¹⁹ when I broke apart the loaves for the five thousand, how many baskets full of leftovers you gathered up?" And they tell him, "Twelve." ²⁰ "And what about the seven loaves for the four thousand, how many baskets full of leftovers did you gather up?" And they say, "Seven" ²¹ So he said to them: "Do you really not yet understand?"

²² And they arrived at Bethsaida and there, people brought to him a blind man asking that he touch him. ²³ So, taking the hand of the blind man, he brought him out of the hamlet, and applying spit to his eyes and laying hands on him, he asked him, "Can you see anything?" ²⁴ And he looked up and was saying, "I see people walking around like trees." ²⁵ Then he laid hands again on his eyes and he opened his eyes and his sight was restored and he was able to see everything clearly. ²⁶ He then sent him home, saying, "Don't enter the hamlet."

Thinking about Mark

One of the barriers to serious engagement by Jews with gentiles related to purity laws and unclean foods. Normally Jews should not frequent gentile homes and dine with them. We see this reflected in the story that Matthew and Luke bring about the centurion seeking healing for his slave (Matt 8:5–13; Luke 7:1–10). After Jesus' response to his request, perhaps best translated: "Am I to come and heal him?" (8:7)—by implication: you surely don't want me to enter a gentile's house, the centurion responds sensitively: "I am not worthy to have you come under my roof" (Matt 8:8), in other words, of course not.

Acts records a story about Peter's initial reluctance to enter Cornelius' house, a gentile, telling him: "You yourselves know that it is unlawful for a Jew to associate with or to visit a Gentile" (10:28). Similarly, Paul expresses anger and disappointment that in response to a delegation from James (Jesus' brother and head of the Jerusalem church), Peter and Barnabas withdrew from regular fellowship meals with gentiles in Antioch (Gal 2:11–14).

If the gospel is to reach out and embrace gentiles, that barrier had to be addressed. Accordingly, Mark has it addressed between the feeding of the five thousand and the feeding of the four thousand. For in Mark 7 he brings another story about conflict between Jesus and Pharisees and scribes like those he had brought in chapters 2 and 3. Conflict arose over the disciples' eating without first washing their hands (7:1–2). The issue was not hygiene but purity. Eating with hands that had become ritually unclean would make the food unclean.

To enable gentiles who might be listening to his gospel to understand the issue, Mark describes the concerns of Jews with issues of purity. They not only wash hands for purposes of ritual purification, but also "cups, pots, and bronze vessels" (7:4). Matters of purification were taken very seriously in first-century Judaism, evident in Galilee, for instance, in archaeological finds that include many stone jars, believed not to be able to be contaminated by impurity, and the large number of immersion pools used for purification.

As with the conflict stories in Mark 2–3, this story in 7:1–23 has probably undergone elaboration and expansion, but underlying it is Jesus' response in 7:15, "Nothing entering a person from outside them can render a person ritually unclean, but it's what comes out of people that makes them dirty." There is play on defecation here. Mark expounds the significance of this response by saying that Jesus was thereby "declaring all foods clean as such" (7:19). This comes after Mark has Jesus appeal to common sense:

food simply enters the stomach and exits into the toilet (7:18–19). How can it possibly make a person unclean! Instead, attitudes of mind inspiring evil actions were what made a person unclean, at least in the sense that Mark considered alone important, namely morally sinful attitudes and actions such as "evil thoughts, sexual immorality, theft, murder, adultery, greed, deceit, lust, envy, slander, pride, and stupidity" (7:21–22).

Perhaps Jesus' original comment was more in the sense of saying: not so much food entering our bodies defiles us as what emanates from our minds, it is a matter of priorities. Mark presents it as more radical and in effect appeals to common sense not just against oral law, which lay behind the elaborate concerns with so much purification, such as of hands, but also against biblical law, the foundation of purity laws generally and of the distinction between clean and unclean food. Mark sees such biblical law as not only no longer applying but as never having made sense. This is a radical stance.

Mark reinforces in this way what Paul and others had argued on the basis of the compassion at the heart of the gospel which, he argued, required that barriers such as requiring circumcision and conformity to food and purity laws be set aside. Love at the heart of the biblical message thus overrode such concerns. The kind of conservatism that wanted to keep such barriers in place because their Bible demanded them, or which went only halfway, and was prepared to set the requirement of circumcision aside but retain barriers against dining with gentiles, as James, Peter, and Barnabas advocated, created major division in the early church. Mark and Paul are radical and consistent. Matthew rewrites this passage to reduce it to a ruling only on oral law about handwashing. He had Jesus declare, after all, that every stroke of biblical law was to be upheld (5:18–19), as did Luke (16:17), who omitted this passage from his gospel along with the feeding of the four thousand.

Between the critics' challenge and Jesus' probably original response in 7:15 along with its elaboration by Mark in what follows, we find additional material reflecting on the conflict. The first has Jesus charge the critics with hypocrisy for putting so much emphasis on such oral laws and neglecting biblical law (7:6–8). In what follows, Mark has Jesus then point to their development of laws, which effectively gave people an excuse not to care for their parents (7:9–13), suggesting that they often manipulated the law in this way, allegations that reflect a history of conflict between the Jesus movement and its critics.

The primary focus and function of the passage in 7:1–23, however, is show how and why the barriers that hindered full engagement with gentiles were to be abandoned and that this was based on Jesus' own teaching (and what Mark seeks to portray as common sense). Matthew and Luke would argue with this, and perhaps they were right, in the sense that originally Jesus' clever saying was about setting priorities among biblical laws not about setting them aside. On the other hand, as already Paul argued, at the heart of the gospel of Jesus was a commitment to inclusivity and compassion, whose logic required such abandonment, a decision Jesus, working primarily with Jews, never needed to confront.

Having depicted Jesus' removing the barriers, indeed, declaring them never to have made sense, Mark inserts into his storyline an anecdote that illustrates Jesus' crossing barriers when confronted with human need in the region of Tyre on the Mediterranean coast, gentile territory (7:24–30). It is somewhat daring, since it starts with having Jesus respond to the woman, a Syrophoenician, so a gentile, in a way that it then has him abandon. She seeks help for her daughter, whose condition Mark depicts in the diagnostic categories typical of his approach, as having an unclean spirit and so needing to be liberated from it.

Jesus' initial response is shocking to us but would have been typical of many in his time: "Let the children be fed first. It is not right to take the children's food and throw it to the dogs" (7:27). We Jews are God's children; by contrast, gentiles are like dogs! This is not said with the sense that we love dogs as pets, "man's best friend," as one used to say. Dogs, here, is a derogatory term. The storytellers from whom Mark eventually received this story were prepared to depict Jesus as expressing such a racist slur. Nothing suggests it was tongue in cheek, as though he did not mean it.

Did Jesus really say something like this? We might want to hope that he didn't, but if he did, it would have reflected his being brought up in a fairly conservative family with a strong sense of Jewish identity, reflected, for instance, in its choice of biblical names for its children, and harboring some extreme attitudes. Were his responses to the leper (if becoming angry is the original text in 1:41) and perhaps to the woman who touched him (5:30) and to the possibility of entering the gentile centurion's house (Matt 8:7) also reflective of such a beginning? Did Jesus have to undergo changes to his attitude?

Mark tells the story not to explore possible prejudices Jesus might have been brought up with, but in order to show him being willing to set them aside. The conservatism is still reflected in his healing the girl at a distance and thus not entering a gentile house (as also in not entering the gentile centurion's house in Matt 8:7–13). For Mark, the main point is that Jesus' willingness to respond to a gentile woman's need foreshadowed and modeled what the movement would need to do: reach out equally to gentiles and their needs with the gospel and the healing it brought.

Mark's use of the story as a model for the future is reflected also in the presence of the word "first" in "Let the children be fed first" (7:27). That reflected the sequence of events as they developed in the Jesus movement after his death and resurrection. We see the sequence reflected for instance in Paul's words in Romans: "For I am not ashamed of the gospel; it is the power of God for salvation to everyone who has faith, to the Jew first and also to the Greek" (1:16).

The woman is a hero. In the story she persuades Jesus to change tack. Humiliating for a man in those times to be corrected by a woman? Yes, probably. She is affirmed. Jesus does not hide behind male obsession with ego dignity but follows the appeal to love. It was, after all, his usual way and the heart of the good news. She says: dogs are usually allowed to pick up the crumbs under the table. Mark has Jesus go into reverse back from his stance and reward her response with a remote expulsion of the demon, but still keeping his Jewish distance as he did in healing the centurion's slave. Despite such hesitant cultural distancing, Mark shows Jesus prioritizing love and liberation. That was enough. In Mark's day it had come to mean much more.

Mark then has Jesus cross back from the coastal regions, but again into gentile territory east of the Sea of Galilee (7:31), and heal a deaf man with a speech impediment, presumably also a gentile. First-century listeners to Mark's Gospel would not have been surprised to hear the description of what Jesus did: "He put his fingers into his ears and with spittle on his fingers touched his tongue. Then looking up to heaven with a sigh, he said, '*Ephphatha!*'—which means 'Be opened!'" (7:33–34). This was first-century medical practice. Spittle was believed to have healing qualities and touch transferred healing powers. In 8:23 he applies it to the eyes of a blind man. Similarly, in John's Gospel we also read of Jesus' use of spittle: "He spat on the ground and made mud with the saliva and spread the mud on the man's eyes" (9:6). The Aramaic word *Ephphatha*, like the use of *talitha cum* when raising Jairus' daughter to life (5:41), would have been heard by some of Mark's hearers as like magic words of power used in spells by healers of the time.

It is possible that Mark is simply adding another miracle to his storyline of Jesus, but its location here may well also be symbolic. In the conversation about the meaning of the feedings of the five thousand and the four thousand Jesus will challenge his disciples about being deaf and blind, in striking contrast to the man here made to hear and then the man in 8:22–26 made to see.

Mark completes his narrative argument for openness to the gentile world by bringing an account of a second mass feeding (8:1–10). It may be his creation for the purpose, or it may have come to him as a separate story or a variant of the first feeding. The disciples' response to the needs of the crowd read as though they had not experienced anything like that before, whereas, according to Mark's storyline, they had, not so long before.

For Mark's purpose, it symbolizes the blessing of the gospel coming to gentiles. He had filled the account of the feeding of the five thousand with images and numbers evocative of Israel: location in Jewish territory; Israel as like "sheep without a shepherd"; setting them down in groups like Israel in the wilderness; the symbolic numbers: twelve, five thousand, five. Now this feeding takes place in gentile territory. The seven loaves and the seven baskets evoked the universal, seven seen as a symbol of completeness, representing all peoples, and four in four thousand evoked the four winds or four corners of the earth. Gentiles too can feast on the good news Jesus brings. Here, too, Jesus has compassion on the crowd. The reference to three days may evoke the Easter story, for only after Easter did the gentile mission really begin.

The sequel, that the Pharisees ask for a sign, seems quite unrelated to the context, unless we take it as another hint that Mark is giving the listeners to his gospel that they should grasp the message he is seeking to convey in these chapters. This may well be so, because what follows is a play on the image of bread. The exhortation to beware of the yeast, the bread, of the Pharisees and Herod (Antipas) makes two connections. First, it recalls Mark's statement in 3:6 that the Pharisees and Herodians conspired together to have Jesus killed. Second, it may reflect on Antipas' feast, which led to John's execution.

As a contrast to that feast, Mark has told how Jesus has fed thousands of Jews and then thousands of gentiles. Now he poses a kind of riddle, challenging them for failing to grasp the significance of what has been happening. "Do you have eyes, and fail to see? Do you have ears, and fail to hear?" (8:18). Those listening to Mark's Gospel have just heard of Jesus helping a man to hear and are just about to hear about Jesus helping a man to see. Would they get the message Mark is wanting them to grasp through pointing to the twelve and the seven baskets? Would they have grasped that Mark was declaring and indeed celebrating the expansion of the good news to reach not only Jews but also gentiles, made possible in part by removal of the barriers, as Mark 7 had indicated?

The disciples appear blind. This is all the more confronting when Mark goes on to tell of Jesus' engaging in a two-step process of healing the blind man in Bethsaida, also using spittle and touch as in the healing the deaf man (8:22–26). The instruction to go home and not return to the village recalls similar instructions given to the leper (1:44), to the witnesses to the raising of Jairus' daughter to life (5:43), and after the healing of the deaf man (7:36), which people ignored. In part the problem was how to cope with thronging crowds. It was also that popular acclamation had the potential to alert rulers like Antipas, who would see him then as a threat. In his storyline Mark is about to embark on the downhill journey to Jesus' demise.

Thus far, Mark has portrayed Jesus as fulfilling his mission, described by John the Baptist as baptizing with the Spirit. By the Spirit's power Jesus has brought healing, portrayed mostly as liberating people from demons. At the same time, he has been teaching, though we find little specific reference to the content of his teaching, beyond the fact that he used parables, and, even then, by using them to assert that his predictions would come true despite setbacks. The predictions are also very general. Mark sums them up as the coming of the kingdom, the reign, of God, and suggests that in part that was beginning to happen as Jesus brought healing and liberation.

From chapter 6 onward Mark has concentrated primarily on the reach of this movement of liberation and hope and, using the imagery of the miraculous feedings, portrays its expansion to include not only Jews but also gentiles. Having done so, Mark moves from midway through Mark 8 to focus primarily on the impending fate of Jesus and in the process brings instruction about disciples and how they should live. Their identity is bound up with the identity of Jesus. Who is Jesus and who are they? Who are they to be? There is also a sense in which Mark is inviting those who will be listening to his gospel, who will mostly be those whose inclusion the feeding of the four thousand celebrates, to reflect on who they are.

Reflection: What issues did the first believers need to face in following through the sharing of good news with all? Why did different approaches to Scripture play such a role? In what ways do you see barriers, biblical and otherwise, creating issues for our being good news today?

— 3 —

The Identity

Who Is He and Who Are We? (8:27—9:13)

Listening to Mark

8:27 And Jesus and his disciples set off from there for the hamlets around Caesarea Philippi and along the way, he was asking his disciples, "Who do people say I am?" **28** They said, "John the Baptist and others say Elijah, and others, one of the prophets." **29** So he asked them, "What about you? Who do you say I am?" Peter replied, "You are the Messiah." **30** And he told them not to tell anyone about him. **31** Then he began to teach them, saying, "The Son of Man must suffer many things and be rejected by the elders and the chief priests and the scribes and be put to death and rise again after three days." **32** He made this statement openly, but Peter took him aside and started to challenge him. **33** He then turned around and looked at his disciples and challenged Peter saying, "Get behind me Satan! You're focusing on human priorities not God's priorities."

34 Then summoning the crowd along with the disciples, he said, "If anyone wants to follow me, let them deny themselves and take up their cross and follow me. **35** Whoever wants to save their life will lose it and whoever loses their life for my sake and the sake of the good news, will save it. **36** For what profit is in it for people to gain the whole world only to lose their life? **37** What will a person give up in exchange for their life? **38** Whoever is ashamed of me and my words in this adulterous and sinful generation, the Son of Man will be ashamed of them when he comes in glory with his holy angels." **9:1** And he told them, "Truly I say to you, there are some standing here who will not taste death before they the kingdom of God having arrived in power."

2 Six days later, Jesus takes Peter and James and John with him up a high mountain on their own and was transformed in front of them. **3** His clothes became shiny white such as no launderer on earth could ever make them. **4** And Elijah appeared before them along with Moses and they were talking with Jesus. **5** Peter's response was to say, "Rabbi, it's great that we can be here. So let's make three tents, one for you, one for Moses and one for Elijah." **6** For he didn't know how to respond, because they were overawed. **7** And a cloud overshadowed them, and a voice spoke out of the cloud, "This is my beloved Son; listen to him!" **8** Then suddenly they looked around and no longer saw anyone with them except Jesus.

9 On the way down the mountain Jesus instructed them not to tell anyone what they had seen until after the Son of Man had risen from the dead. **10** So they kept the matter to themselves and wondered what was this rising from the dead comment was about. **11** He was asking them, "The scribes say that Elijah must come first, don't they?" **12** He continued, "Well, yes, Elijah will come and restore everything, but how come then it is written that the Son of Man has to suffer many things and be rejected? **13** Well, let me tell you, Elijah has in fact come and they did to him whatever they pleased, as is written about him."

Thinking about Mark

Following his pattern for doing things in pairs, Mark follows up his first mention of people wondering who Jesus was when introducing Antipas' wonderings (6:14–16) with a second such occasion, now located far to the north at Caesarea Philippi (8:27–28), around twenty-five miles (forty kilometers) north of the Sea of Galilee. People's guesses as reported by the disciples are the same as then: John the Baptist, Elijah, or one of the prophets. Indeed, there was an expectation among some that Elijah would return (Mal 4:5–6). He had, after all, ascended to heaven in a whirlwind, according to the legend (2 Kgs 2:11), which meant he was still in some way alive in the heavenly realms. Moses had predicted that God would raise up a prophet like himself, according to Deuteronomy 18:15. Such expectations were alive in early Judaism and they will find an echo very shortly in Mark's account of Jesus' gloriously transformed appearance on the mountain, where he appears alongside Elijah and Moses (9:4).

Mark has Jesus ask the disciples how they viewed him, and Peter acclaimed: "You are the Messiah" (8:29). But what did that mean—then and in Mark's time? Our first clue comes in Jesus' stern response to tell no one. Why? Almost certainly because it would have been dangerous. People who claimed to be the Messiah were likely to face execution. Mark's first-century listeners knew the end of the story: this is exactly what happened to Jesus. He was crucified under the charge "King of the Jews," a title of the Messiah.

As noted earlier, Messiah is the English version of the Hebrew word meaning the Anointed, its Greek equivalent being *Christos*, also coming through into English, as the Christ. It became the key claim made about Jesus after which members of his movement were called Christians. But what did it mean? When used of future hope, it meant an anointed king like David, thus sometimes called the Son of David and clearly the King of the Jews, the King of Israel. He could also be called the Son of God, as kings were adopted as God's sons to reign on God's behalf.

If those were the familiar titles, the expectation of what the Messiah might do varied. While we sometimes find expectation of a priestly Messiah, sometimes alongside a royal one, the most common expectation was that this coming king would lead an army to liberate Israel from its Roman occupiers. Josephus tells us of such men, hailed as the Messiah, and leading militia. When Pilate executed Jesus as would-be Messiah, he put him broadly into the same category of subversion. Hence, his crucifying Jesus alongside two other subversives, sometimes mistakenly described as thieves. They were revolutionaries. This is also why Pilate offered to swap Jesus for Barabbas, a rebel leader.

To be called a Messiah was seriously dangerous. Mark has Jesus not only tell people not to speak of it, but also has him go on to give the title a distinctive meaning, speaking of himself as Son of Man. He would face suffering and be rejected by the elders, chief priests, and scribes, and be killed. For most people embracing hope for a Messiah, this was the opposite of what was meant to happen. A Messiah wins; he doesn't lose. Peter agreed and so took Jesus aside to correct him. In a dramatic turnaround, Jesus rebukes Peter in front of the rest of the disciples, telling him he's aligned with Satan and has bought into typical human values not God's values.

Peter had got it so wrong according to Mark. This is somewhat astonishing given Peter's senior position among the disciples and his status later, but fully understandable in the light of normal hopes and expectations associated with someone being the Messiah. Mark is happy to have Jesus acclaimed as Messiah but only as long as people understood Messiah in a very different way. Mark has him accept being called the Messiah, but only on his own terms. Mark's Jesus sees himself as the messianic Son of Man set on a path of suffering leading to death from which God would raise him back to life three days later. Earlier, we noted that in his role as Messiah/Son of Man Jesus would exercise authority to conduct judgment at the climax of history.

Mark, therefore, has Jesus challenge prevailing values which assumed that following God's way meant winning, success, victory. Instead, God's way is suffering. It is not meaningless suffering. It is suffering as a result of seeking to be a bearer of God's agenda, God's compassion. In this sense, it also challenges our understanding of God or at least of where we see God. To say that we see God where compassion is exercised, to see God as love and loving, is to subvert models of God that see God's greatness primarily in terms of power and control, projections onto God of popular human models of mighty kings. What does it mean to be truly great?

Mark develops this theme over the chapters that follow. He has Jesus repeat his prediction twice more that as Son of Man he would face rejection and death (9:31; 10:33–34). Mark sometimes chooses to do things in threes. On each of these occasions he depicts the disciples as failing to grasp Jesus' values. In chapter 9 he shows them arguing about who would be the greatest and in chapter 10 he reports how James and John want pride of place in power beside Jesus in a conversation that concludes with Jesus' making it very clear: "For the Son of Man did not come to be served but to serve and to give his life a ransom for many" (10:45).

Mark's redefined image of Jesus as Messiah would have also spoken to his own day and helped quell suspicions that the Jesus movement was a political threat to imperial rule and accordingly to be suppressed. Mark does not stop at having Jesus clarify in what sense he could be called Messiah. He also has Jesus address the implications of such values for the disciples and has Jesus draw the crowds in to listen (8:34–37).

Jesus in Mark's Gospel challenges any who want to be his followers to be prepared to deny themselves and even face death on a cross, as he would. At one level, Mark's Jesus here would be speaking as much to Mark's own day when people may have faced serious danger from the state. At another level, the challenge is about how one sees oneself.

To choose to follow Jesus is also of course a decision people make because it is what they decide they want to do and so will not deny themselves in that sense by not doing so. Here in this saying the assumption is that to follow self is to act solely in one's own interest at the expense of others or even to endeavor to sustain a false sense of self artificially created to win affection and behind which to hide one's true self. Greatness or finding one's true self is about embracing love from and for God, for others, and for oneself.

"For my sake and the sake of the good news" indicates the prospect of suffering as a believer, but the broader sense also comes through. It appeals in that sense to self-interest, not to lose one's life. The adjacent saying about gaining the whole world and losing oneself also has broad application.

Mark has Jesus round off these comments with reference to Jesus' future role as the Son of Man. It is the first such reference but has been assumed from the beginning. Mark shares the expectation that the risen Jesus will return to exercise a role in the judgment.

Mark goes on to have Jesus declare that this would occur within the lifetime of Jesus' hearers: "Truly I say to you, there are some standing here who will not taste death before they the kingdom of God having arrived in power" (9:1). People endeavor to explain away its failure to come about by suggesting that Mark must have meant the transfiguration of Jesus just about to be recounted or actions to show God's reign breaking in through Jesus or in the early church. The more natural reading is to hear in it Mark's sharing an assumption of his day that history would soon reach its end. Paul, too, had assumed it would occur during his lifetime, when he speaks of those still alive, including himself, at Jesus' coming joining those to be raised from the dead (1 Thess 4:15).

There was a widespread assumption that history would have to come to an end soon, given the plight in which most people found themselves. Our assumptions about time do not match theirs, just as our assumptions about the earth, the age of creation, do not match theirs. Nearly two thousand years have passed, and we are still going! Their wisdom was clothed in

THE IDENTITY

their assumptions. To recognize this does not mean they lacked wisdom; it means we need to hear that wisdom and express it in our terms.

The focus on history's climax and the return of Jesus in glory continues in the account of Jesus' ascending a high mountain with his inner group of disciples, Peter, James, and John (9:2–8). Mountains were often seen as ways of rising up to be close to God, a widely held symbolism. Moses ascended Mount Sinai to receive the ten commandments, indeed also after six days, as here (Exod 24:16), probably an intentional allusion.

The scene to follow is a foretaste of what would happen at Jesus' return. The book of Daniel pictures the resurrected at the climax of history shining like stars in the sky (12:3). The scene therefore shows Jesus in the way Mark imagines he will appear, shining with closeness to the divine. There are probably multiple allusions, as often in such symbolic scenes. Moses' face shone on Mount Sinai (Exod 34:29). Jesus appears with Elijah, who has already been the focus of attention in the disciples' reports of what people were wondering about Jesus' identity and the issue of Elijah's identity will return as they go down from the mountain. The focus on Elijah explains why the mention of Moses is almost secondary, but Moses or a prophet like Moses was also part of some popular imaginings of history's climax. Sometimes it was, indeed, the Messiah accompanied by Moses and Elijah.

Some have wondered if Mark means us to think of the Law and the Prophets, represented by Moses and Elijah, and have suggested that Mark's symbolic story is about continuing with Israel's tradition. This cannot be ruled out, but the context is clearly about the end of time and the focus on Elijah in the expression "Elijah with Moses" (instead of Moses and Elijah) and the subsequent conversation about Elijah's role at the climax of history confirms that the primarily focus is the end time. Mark is giving us an advance glimpse of how he sees Jesus' return of which he had just spoken at the end of the previous chapter.

Mark has the three disciples in this symbolic scene overwhelmed by what they saw and responding with plans to house all three, perhaps to ensure that they stay. One might smile at the detail many centuries later when we encounter people almost obsessed with buildings, but that is not Mark's intent here. He has the disciples simply having no idea what was happening until, as in the symbolic narrative of Jesus' baptism, a voice comes from heaven out of a cloud: "This is my beloved Son; listen to him!" (9:7). Unlike at the baptism these words are addressed to the disciples and, Mark implies, to all disciples. "Listen to him!" In this sense it is a challenge to take note of the teaching of Jesus which Mark will bring in the chapters which follow.

Mark's story of the heavenly voice identifying Jesus as God's Son is the second of another set of three. The first occasion was at his baptism and the final occasion is when the voice comes not from God above but from below, from a gentile centurion: "Truly this man was God's Son!" (15:39).

Once the vision disappeared and Jesus and his three disciples were on their way down the mountain, the focus on the end time continued with the discussion about Elijah, expected to herald the coming of the Messiah (9:9–13). It ends with an allusion to John the Baptist as fulfilling Elijah's role. Mark's flexibility of thought allowed him to see John bearing the spirit of Elijah, something some had speculated might be the case with Jesus, himself, when they identified him with Elijah (6:14–16). In that sense, the conversation brings us back in typical style of authors of the time to where this section began in 8:27–30, and again, as there, we have Jesus commanding that the disciples keep quiet about his identity until after his resurrection.

Reflection: Why was calling Jesus the Messiah both dangerous and potentially distorting and how was it tweaked to fit gospel priorities? How do we deal with the fact that the climax of history and Jesus' return did not happen in the lifetime of the first disciples?

THE IDENTITY

Demons and Disciples (9:14–50)

Listening to Mark

¹⁴ Returning to the rest of the disciples, they saw a big crowd around them and scribes arguing with them. ¹⁵ When they saw him, the crowd was immediately amazed and ran over to welcome him. ¹⁶ And he asked them, "Why were you arguing with them?" ¹⁷ And one of the crowd responded, "Teacher, I have brought my son to you who has a spirit that prevents him talking. ¹⁸ And wherever it takes hold of him, it throws him on the ground, and he foams at the mouth and grinds his teeth and becomes all stiff. And I told your disciples to get them to expel it, but they didn't have the capacity." ¹⁹ Jesus replied, "O faithless generation, how long do I have to be with you! How long must I put up with you! Bring him here to me."

²⁰ And they brought him to him and, seeing him, the spirit immediately convulsed him and he fell to the ground rolling around foaming at the mouth. ²¹ And he asked his father, "How long has this been going on?" He said, "Since he was a child. ²² And often it throws him even into the fire and into water to try to kill him. But if you can, have compassion on us and help us!" ²³ Jesus then said to him, "As far as what I can do, everything is possible for a person who has faith." ²⁴ The child's father then exclaimed, "I have faith! Help me with my lack of it!" ²⁵ When Jesus saw that the crowd was running over, he rebuked the unclean spirit, saying, "Dumb and deaf spirit, I command you, leave him and don't enter him ever again!" ²⁶ And crying out and convulsing the child, the spirit left him, and he became like a corpse, so that many said, "He's dead." ²⁷ But Jesus took him by the hand and lifted him up and he got up.

²⁸ When he returned to the house, his disciples asked him on their own, "Why couldn't we expel it?" ²⁹ And he said, "Nothing will get this kind out except prayer." ³⁰ And they went off from there through Galilee and he didn't want anyone to know his whereabouts ³¹ because he was giving instruction to his disciples and telling them,

"The Son of Man will be betrayed into the hands of people who will kill him and having been killed he will rise after three days." ³² But they did not understand what he was saying and were afraid to ask him.

³³ So they came to Capernaum, and when he got home, he asked them, "What were you arguing about on the road?" ³⁴ They remained silent, because they had been arguing with one another about which of them was the greatest. ³⁵ Sitting down, he called the twelve and said to them, "If you want to be first, you will be last of all and servant of all." ³⁶ And taking a little child, he stood him in their midst and putting his arms around him, he said, ³⁷ "Whoever welcomes one such child in my name welcomes me. And whoever welcomes me, welcomes not me but the one who sent me."

³⁸ John told him, "Teacher, we saw someone casting out demons in your name and we tried to stop him, because he wasn't following us." ³⁹ Jesus said, "Don't try to stop him. No one exercising power in my name can turn quickly to malign me. ⁴⁰ Whoever is not against me is for me. ⁴¹ Whoever gives you a cup of water to drink on the basis that you belong to the Messiah, I tell you, will surely not lose their reward.

⁴² And whoever causes one of these little ones who believe in me to stumble, it would be better for them to have a millstone put around their neck and be cast into the sea. ⁴³ And if your hand causes you to stumble, cut it off. Better to enter life disabled than to have two hands and go off into Gehenna, to everlasting fire. ⁴⁵ And if your foot causes you to stumble, cut it off. Better to enter life disabled than to have two feet and go off into Gehenna, to everlasting fire. ⁴⁷ And if your eye causes you to stumble, pluck it out. Better to enter the kingdom of God with one eye than with two and be thrown into Gehenna, ⁴⁸ where their worm never dies, and the fire is never quenched. ⁴⁹ Everyone will be salted with fire. Salt is good, ⁵⁰ but if it becomes unsalty, how are you going to make it salty again? Have salt among yourselves and be at peace with one another."

Thinking about Mark

Mark brings us back to issues of ministry as he understood both Jesus' and the disciples' ministry (9:14–29). He focuses, in particular, therefore, on exorcism, a key element in the commission to baptize people with the

Spirit, as John the Baptist had put it, namely as liberating people from the powers that oppressed them. In an unusually long account, Mark tells of the problem that had arisen when the disciples—apart from Peter, James, and John—were confronted with a situation they could not handle. They were not able to expel a demon from a boy who was unable to speak. The account gives dramatic detail about how the demon used to convulse the boy. Jesus succeeds and lifts up the boy who had looked like he was dead. Mark has Jesus explain to his puzzled disciples that in such difficult cases prayer was necessary.

The account reminds us of how distant that world is from ours and in that sense how alien Jesus is from what we have come to understand as normal. With more detail we might wonder if this was epilepsy. Mark presents us with a strange Jesus and through this account reminds us that this was how he saw Jesus: primarily as an exorcist who claimed such healings were a foretaste of the ultimate overcoming of all evil forces and the establishment of God's reign alone. Beyond the strangeness, we might find connection with the notion that God's will and God's Spirit are about liberating people from the powers that oppress them, even though we do not personalize those powers in the language of demonology.

It is easier for us to relate to the dangers that Mark goes on to show us when he juxtaposes Jesus' mission of lowly and confronting compassion, which would land him in rejection and death, and the disciples' preoccupation with who among them was the greatest (9:30–37). There is nothing strange or remote about that for us. Mark shows Jesus confronting their ambitious values by bringing before them a small child. The assumption is that the child has not yet reached the stage where it had to compete for love. That can happen very early: "My toys! Not yours!" Fear of missing out, especially when a child really does miss out, generates strategies of claiming for oneself and denying others, wanting to be greatest or get the greatest attention and affection. Drop it, argues Jesus.

Mark portrays Jesus as arguing for a different value system where what is valued is caring, including lowly caring. It is in part the language of slavery, but the focus is not forced labor but willing service. In that sense, what might seem on the world's value system to be least and lowliest is subversively called greatness and greatest. This is an invitation to choose that value system, to see it as in one's best interests not to compete against others but to be a person aligned with love, and so with the way that Jesus was and God is. When you then, in turn, welcome such a person who is loving, you are indeed embracing Jesus and God.

The key to being enabled to do so is love. Believing and knowing that you really are loved frees you from fearing you might miss out and so must compete against others. We can see it in young children where they have the sense that there really is enough love to go round. In the broader sense of the gospel, we see it when people take love on board and so become liberated from the almost demonic fear that they will miss out, a fear that can lead to all kinds of strategies to win love from others by creating false selves and mounting winning cases that say: you ought to admire me and surrender to my power. Paul goes furthest in explaining that love sets people free, so that in turn they can bear the fruit of love toward others. Guilt and fear, our demons, which generate division and strife, can be disempowered and love can rule.

Mark concluded the passage about the disciples' obsession with greatness by having Jesus speak of welcoming those who abandon such obsessions and choose love. This apparently prompted him to tell another story that probably had application more in Mark's own day than in the time of Jesus (9:38–41). It perhaps reflects a situation in the growing church where groups might develop separately and then meet and wonder about acceptance of each other. Quasi-denominationalism began very early in the church's life.

In any case, Mark has Jesus calm John's worry about this unfamiliar exorcist who was expelling demons in Jesus' name. The priority is not claiming copyright, as it were, but bringing liberation and healing—for Mark, that means by exorcism. That is the "control" that matters. Otherwise, group control—you have to join *us!*—can be another form of the competition spirit that can stand in the way of love. In our day there are many individuals and groups who bring the liberating love and compassion we see in Jesus to people's lives, sometimes wearing a Christian label and sometimes not, but all of whom we may embrace as sharing oneness in love.

Mark has Jesus go on to warn against abuse of "one of these little ones who believe in me" (9:42). It is not entirely clear what is meant by "these little ones." Mark may be using it metaphorically and mean anyone who believes in Jesus with the humble spirit of a child, as he had in mentioning welcoming "one such child" in 9:37.

On the other hand, Mark's hearers may still have the picture of the little child in their minds, as introduced in 9:36, and so take the warning as against child abuse within the believing community. For Mark will go on to deal with other social matters, like divorce and welcoming children. The striking severity of the warning—being dumped in the sea with a millstone around one's neck—suggests that at least earlier the focus was actual child abuse, something widespread in Mark's world.

The warnings that follow, which employ graphic imagery about cutting off hands and limbs and plucking out eyes (9:43–48), suggest serious sin. Matthew independently knows them as belonging under the category of sexual wrongdoing (5:29–30) and such is probably their meaning here. Causing someone to "stumble" was language sometimes used of sexual wrongdoing.

The warnings threaten hellfire to those not heeding them. Like the threat of being drowned in the depths and the reference to being salted with fire, these warnings function to supplement the appeal to not abuse. Threatening punishment has long been used to motivate change of behavior, but it comes as a very weak second to the appeal to love, care, and respect others, and at worst becomes itself a form of abuse.

The salt saying (9:49–50) defies our science but reflects the practice of using "salt" incorporated with other substances in a mixture in which the actual salt content could be diminished by being washed out and so no longer serve its purpose. It was a useful image of the need to retain quality, to remain committed to love and compassion, and not to allow oneself to be rendered no longer good news to those around you. It includes the idea of being a person who promotes peace and good health in relationships.

Reflection: What do you think Mark was doing in the way he portrayed the disciples and how do you see such behavior manifesting itself today?

Divorce, Remarriage, and Children (10:1-16)

Listening to Mark

¹⁰∶¹ From there they set off for the area of Judea and the Transjordan and again, crowds came to him and as was his custom, he engaged in teaching them. ² Pharisees approached him with the question, "Is it lawful for a man to divorce his wife," a test question. ³ He replied, "What command did Moses give you?" ⁴ They replied, "Moses permitted the man to issue a divorce certificate and divorce his wife." ⁵ Jesus responded, "It was because of your hardness of heart that he wrote that commandment for you. ⁶ But from the beginning of creation 'he made them male and female. ⁷ Therefore a man will leave his father and mother and be joined to his wife ⁸ and the two will become one flesh.' So they are no longer two but one flesh. ⁹ What God has joined together let no human being split apart."

¹⁰ And back in the house, the disciples asked him about this ¹¹ and he said, "Whoever divorces his wife and marries another commits adultery against her ¹² and if she divorces her husband and marries another she commits adultery."

¹³ And people were bringing children to him for him to touch them, but the disciples told them off. ¹⁴ When Jesus saw that, he was angry and said to them, "Let the children come to me. Don't hinder them, for the kingdom of God belongs to such children. ¹⁵ Truly I tell you, whoever does not welcome the kingdom of God like a child, will never enter it." ¹⁶ And taking them into his arms, he laid hands on them and blessed them.

Thinking about Mark

The focus on human relations continues in the first section of chapter 10 where Mark has Jesus address the issue of divorce. In his storyline he has also brought Jesus from Galilee, in the north, down south to Judea and to Perea on the other side of the Jordan River. Mark suggests that some Pharisees confronted Jesus with the issue of divorce to put him on the spot, as it were, because it must have been an area of significant debate. Later rabbinic tradition reports that about the time of Jesus, and before, there were differences among Jewish teachers about what were and what were not acceptable grounds for divorce, usually by a man of a woman.

As long as polygyny (having more than one wife) was widely accepted, one response to marital struggle was for a man to take another wife without necessarily divorcing his first wife. The stories of the patriarchs—Abraham, Isaac, and Jacob—assume polygyny, as do later stories such as those of David and, notoriously, Solomon with his large harem. In the world of the Greeks and the Romans and their cultures, which through conquest influenced life in the Jewish world, monogyny (having one wife) was the norm. Some movements within Judaism advocated monogyny. The Temple Scroll, written perhaps two centuries before Jesus, required monogyny of kings, but other writings, such as those of the Jewish sect of the Essenes whose library was found hidden in caves near the Dead Sea, demanded it of all. There were probably also economic grounds why polygyny was unrealistic, especially for people with limited means.

If you rule out polygyny, then the alternative option when things go awry in a marriage was divorce. It seems that some men were divorcing their wives for trivial reasons. It drove some women into poverty or had them seeking security with their family where that was possible or had them finding other means to survive, which for some meant prostitution.

The Jewish teachers associated with the School of Hillel took a very liberal approach, allegedly even accepting that bad cooking might justify a man's divorcing his wife. The more conservative School of Shammai argued that the grounds had to be serious, such as sexual wrongdoing. Roman law, reinforced by Emperor Augustus, just two decades before Jesus' time, required divorce where adultery had taken place and required that men who refused to divorce their wives when the latter had committed adultery should be prosecuted.

It is then not surprising to find Jesus confronted with the issue. He will have also had to deal with it in the case of Herod Antipas' divorce of his wife and his marrying Herodias who had divorced from his stepbrother, Herod Philip. One might imagine that Mark would have in mind that the issue would also be relevant for those listening to his gospel.

Jesus' response begins by acknowledging the biblical provision for divorce, which is mentioned indirectly in Deuteronomy 24, where the ruling is given that it was forbidden for a man to take back a wife whom he had divorced and who had married another. In the ruling we find the incidental detail that at divorce the man normally gave the woman a certificate of divorce (24:1). This enabled her to remarry. Jesus attributes the ruling to Moses, reflecting the belief of the time that Moses, himself, was the direct source of the rules and commandments found in the first five books of the Hebrew Bible, Genesis to Deuteronomy. We now recognize them as the product of combining centuries of legal tradition, only some of which if any go back to the historical figure of Moses.

Mark's Jesus suggests that this divorce provision was a compromise and should never have been needed. It was introduced because of failure, "hardness of heart" (10:5). Jesus justifies this claim by pointing to the standard texts cited when Jews of the time referred to marriage and its origins, namely the story of the creation of man and woman in Genesis. God made male and female (Gen 1:27) and mandated marriage as coming into being when a man left his family and joined to become one with his wife (Gen 2:24). Jesus reinforces the implication of the text, adding, "So they are no longer two, but one flesh" (10:8). His argument is then stated with simplicity: "What God has joined together let no human being split apart" (10:9).

It is another example of a simple two-part punchline with which Jesus often brought such conflicts to a conclusion, as Mark portrays them. The saying is striking because it contrasts God and human beings. Human beings should not undo what God has done. When I hear farmers talk about "joining" in relation to cattle, they mean mating, sexual intercourse in human terms. When in Genesis 2:24 it refers to the man being joined to the woman and becoming one flesh with her, this refers to sexual union. When Mark has Jesus refer to God's joining the two, it implies that their joining is done according to divine order. It should not then be undone.

Marriage in those days took place as a result of negotiation between families, normally fathers. They arranged the marriage. Most men married around thirty and married girls half their age. An indirect result of this was that many men concluded that their wives were not only less experienced, but also less able to control their feelings and were basically inferior to men. They were, therefore, deemed not fit for public office, but best confined to domestic duties, a prejudice that has survived the centuries. Their understanding of marriage was very different from ours.

The oneness of marriage took place when after the ceremony they consummated their marriage, that is, they had sexual intercourse. This sense of the sexual joining of two people together also helps explain why that union was deemed destroyed when a man or woman joined another in adultery.

The disciples asked Jesus then to unpack the implications of his response and, as the answer, Mark brings a saying that we find in variant form also in other sources. It meant no divorce. In Mark's version, adapted to fit Roman norms where women could also divorce husbands, the prohibition reads: "Whoever divorces his wife and marries another commits adultery against her; and if she divorces her husband and marries another, she commits adultery" (10:11–12).

Remarriage after divorce had to be seen as adultery if the understanding was that the first marriage could not be dissolved. No divorce had, therefore, to mean no remarriage after divorce. The words, "against her," reflect an unusual concern about the woman, unusual in men's discourse of the time. Although Mark probably assumes standard Roman law, namely that divorce must occur if adultery has taken place and that implies that remarriage would then not be adultery, he does not name it.

Matthew's variation of the saying, on the other hand, both when he takes up Mark's story (19:9) and when he cites the prohibition independently (5:32), does reflect the standard law. In both he mentions the exception, "except for sexual immorality," understood as referring primarily to adultery. Neither Luke nor Paul in their versions (1 Cor 7:10–11; Luke 16:18) mentions the exception, though they, too, will have been aware of it and assumed it.

Paul cites the prohibition when confronting the situation in Corinth where marital conflict, indeed, incompatibility, arose when one partner joined the movement and the other did not. He urged them to stay together, but then allowed that for some, divorce would be appropriate (1 Cor 7:12–16). This was typical of Paul's practical flexibility where what governed his ethics was what was most caring in the context. Paul did not see Jesus' words as infallible law that a more appropriate and loving response in some contexts could never overrule. Most today would follow Paul's flexibility while doing everything to try to help marriages work through premarriage education and marriage counselling.

Mark follows the account of Jesus' response to the divorce question with a story about attitudes toward children (10:13–16). Parents came with their children, bringing them to Jesus that he might touch them, and the disciples tell them off. Some among those listening to Mark's Gospel might still have in their minds Jesus' warning about sexual abuse of children and see the disciples' action as justified on those grounds. The word translated "little child" was also used for adolescent children, as for Jairus' twelve-year-old daughter in 5:41–42, an age when such children were extremely vulnerable. Some teachers were notorious sexual predators. "Touch" was a word that often had sexual connotations, as it has in Paul's letter to the Corinthians (1 Cor 7:1). Some of Mark's hearers might have imagined such a scenario.

Mark does not read it this way but appears rather to suggest that the disciples' concern was that people should not bother Jesus by bringing their children to him. He has Jesus rebuke the disciples and instead take the children into his arms and lay his hands on them—but to bless them. His words, "whoever does not receive the kingdom of God as a little child will never enter it" (10:15), make a connection back to his teaching about lowliness in the previous chapter (9:33–36). Children before the stage when they feel they need to compete for love are the model to follow, especially if you can convince yourself that there really is enough love to go around.

Both the anecdote about divorce and that about children will have been told and retold to deal with life in the early church communities. They assume that normal human life as created by God was to be lived out in families, almost certainly also in monogamous families, that is, having one husband and one wife. Mark has no further stories dealing with broader issues that might interest us, such as living with teenagers, gender diversity, same-gender marriage, sexual abuse generally. However, as we shall see next, he does have Jesus address issues of poverty and wealth.

Reflection: Why was divorce an issue and why did marriage matter? What priorities do we bring to marriage crises today and how do we ensure gospel values prevail? What has changed and what has not changed in the way we understand marriage, family, and children between our world and theirs?

THE IDENTITY

Confronting Wealth and Poverty (10:17–31)

Listening to Mark

¹⁷ And as he was heading off on his way, a man came running up to him, knelt in front of him, and asked, "Good teacher, what do I need to do to inherit eternal life?" ¹⁸ Jesus replied, "Why do you call me good? No one is good but God alone. ¹⁹ You know the commandments, do not murder, do not commit adultery, do not steal, do not bear false witness, do not defraud, honor your father and mother." ²⁰ He replied, "Teacher, I have kept all these since my youth." ²¹ Jesus, looking at him, loved him, and said to him, "You're missing one thing. Go, sell what you have and give the proceeds to the poor, and you will have treasure in heaven, and come, follow me." ²² But he was disheartened at this comment and went off feeling sad because he had many possessions.

²³ Looking around, Jesus says to his disciples, "How difficult it is for people with wealth to enter the kingdom of God." ²⁴ The disciples were amazed at his comments, so Jesus responded again, saying, "Children, how hard it is to enter the kingdom of God. ²⁵ It is easier for a camel to pass through the eye of a needle than for a rich person to enter the kingdom of God." ²⁶ They were all the more perplexed and began to say to each other, "Who then can be saved?" ²⁷ Jesus, looking at them, says, "Impossible for human beings; but not for God. Everything is possible for God." ²⁸ Peter began to say to him, "Look, we have abandoned everything and followed you." ²⁹ Jesus responded, "Truly I tell you, there is no one who has left behind their household or brothers or sisters or mother or father for my sake and the sake of the good news ³⁰ who will not receive a hundredfold in this age of brothers, sisters, mothers, and children, and farms, along with persecution, and, in the age to come, eternal life. ³¹ Many who are first will be last and the last, first."

Thinking about Mark

Mark follows his depiction of Jesus' teaching about children, marriage, and divorce, with an anecdote about wealth. For Mark's first hearers it will have had relevance, as it still has, but it could also be easily misunderstood.

Mark does not tell us initially that the man who approached Jesus was rich. He was simply a person wanting "to inherit eternal life" (10:17). That could mean something like: go to heaven, but Mark probably means much more. It was the fundamental question about life, both now and in the future, and we might say, about sharing God's life. Similarly, the question put in other terms, "What must I do to be saved?," needs to be understood in a much broader sense than sometimes assumed when people to reduce it to: how can I avoid going to hell?

Jesus' response does not initially answer the question but takes up the words with which the man had addressed him, "Good teacher," doubtless expressed in sincerity. "Why do you call me good? No one is good but God alone" is confronting. Did Jesus perhaps object to a sense of being patronized by the man? This is possible, but he certainly shifts attention from himself to God. Contrary to much popular piety, Jesus does not show himself in his ministry as engaged primarily in self-promotion and seeking adulation, much as this can sometimes happen among church leaders. Jesus puts God at the center, not himself.

Matthew, sensitive to the possibility that someone might conclude that Jesus was saying he was bad, reworks the dialogue so that Jesus now says: "Why do you ask me about what is good?" (19:17). When he reuses the story, Luke leaves it unchanged (18:19). Jesus follows his pointing the man in God's direction and away from himself by adding reference to the commandments (Mark 10:19). This was what any well-informed Jew would also have answered and there is no reason to imagine that Jesus thought otherwise. To share God's life meant keeping the commandments.

Both Matthew and Luke must have observed that the list of commandments that Mark has Jesus give includes one that is not in the Ten Commandments, namely, "Do not defraud," so they omit it (Matt 19:18–19; Luke 18:19–20). Matthew also reshapes them to match the formulation in the biblical listing, changing "Do not . . ." to "You shall not . . ." and adds "Also, You shall love your neighbor as yourself" (19:19). Mark goes on to tell us that the man assured Jesus: "Teacher, I have kept all these since my youth" (10:20). Matthew drops the words "from my youth" and instead depicts him as a young man and then playfully has Jesus tell him what he

THE IDENTITY

needed to do if he wants to grow up (using a word that has a range of meaning including mature, complete, and perfect; 19:20).

Mark's story tells us that Jesus looked at him with affection (10:21), clearly not showing any sign that he thought the man was not genuine. Both Matthew and Luke delete reference to Jesus' affection, probably in order to sharpen the difference between the two. We might smile when we hear Jesus' words to the man: "You're missing one thing"—especially when we know he apparently lacked nothing, since he was rich. The "one thing" lacking becomes clear when Jesus challenges him to sell his possessions and come and follow him.

It is possible to read the story as if Mark means that only by following Jesus could one have eternal life. Then the one thing lacking was following Jesus. That, however, amounts to saying that Jesus' first answer to the man's quest was incorrect and that following Jesus needed to be added. This is not likely. Rather, what the man lacked was exposed when he refused to sell his possessions and follow the way Jesus read the commandments, namely not as rules to keep, ticking boxes, but as ways to live out compassion and love. Following Jesus was not an alternative way to salvation. It was to keep the commandments the Jesus way and the way that those who read them from their heart would have interpreted them.

If your keeping the commandments is not good news for the poor, then something is indeed lacking. Mark's brief story exposes that gap. By challenging the man to surrender his wealth and give to the poor, Jesus challenged him to see faith in a new way. Many people who never do wrong may rarely do good. Matthew sought to reinforce the underlying value of the commandments by having Jesus cite Leviticus also: "and you shall love your neighbor as yourself" (Matt 19:19).

Luke sees the connection clearly and has this story also help shape his introduction to the parable of Good Samaritan in Luke 10. He takes the man's question (18:18) and reuses it on the lips of Jewish lawyer (10:25), to which he has Jesus answer as Jesus does later, according to Mark, namely by citing the two greatest commandments (Mark 12:28–24). The message is the same: the way to eternal life is to be a neighbor to people in need, for that is to share God's life.

Mark tells us that the man refused to take up the challenge and went away sad (10:22). How would people listening to Mark's story have felt? Most lived in villages, in families, in houses, some in poverty, but all with some possessions needed for life. Was Mark wanting them all to feel bad by suggesting that they should sell up, give money from their sales to the poor, and hit the streets to live in poverty? Almost certainly not. Nor was that the case during Jesus' ministry. He called some to hit the road with him and live on others' generosity, and called this rich man to do so; but most people he called to live out their faith at home. Otherwise, the movement would not have survived. By Mark's time it comprised groups meeting in houses that members owned, with only an occasional visit from itinerants who had hit the road to be envoys.

Whether on the road with Jesus tripping around Galilee or staying at home in one of its villages, whether an envoy darting about the eastern Mediterranean on mission or being a member of a local congregation in your town or village, the challenge of the gospel remained the same according to Mark: to be good news for the poor, to share the life of God by keeping the commandment in the spirit in which Jesus interpreted them, and to look forward in hope to a vision of justice and peace for all peoples.

Mark was sensitive to the issues that Jesus' response to the rich man raised and so appends to the story some discussion of its implications (10:23–31). He has Jesus press home the point about the basic conflict between hanging on to possessions, being bad news for the poor, and engaging in God's reign of love, being good news for the poor. He suggests it is as hard as trying to thread a camel through a needle's eye! There have been many ways of escaping the challenge, from claiming possessions as God's blessing and reward to claiming that faith is only about the soul and its future salvation not about issues such as poverty and injustice, let alone poverty in a broader sense of disadvantage, disability, and discrimination.

Impossible! Especially, if read as a prerequisite for entering God's kingdom in the life to come. Who could possible qualify? When Mark has Jesus declare it possible because God makes it so, Mark doubtless does not mean that God engages in a kind of mathematical gymnastics that would end with a plus figure. He does mean that we need to see God as loving and generous. Love makes a way, but not by false arithmetic. This is not about calculation, as though for God to give us hope would mean needing to fabricate grounds through some kind of manipulation (for instance, by having someone else take the punishment otherwise due to us, as some have interpreted the death of Jesus). God does not need justification or being paid off to be able to love. Love loves.

Mark's Jesus reassures Peter and the anxious disciples with love that defies arithmetic. They will reap a hundred times what they have lost.

Again, this is imagery and exaggeration. The reality is that Jesus has persuaded them that it is indeed in their interests, and the best way to lead a fulfilled life, to join oneself to love, to share God's life and love in the world. In this way, by merging love of God, love of neighbor, and love of self as one, and not as competing options mutually depriving one another, one finds life, indeed, eternal life.

Reflection: What does Mark highlight as the difference between Jesus and the rich man in the way they understood keeping the commandments? What does it mean to be good news for the poor in our world?

Wanting to Be Top Dogs (10:32–52)

Listening to Mark

³² When they were on the road up to Jerusalem with Jesus leading the way, they were amazed and those following were afraid. Taking the twelve aside again, he began to tell them what was going to happen: ³³ "Look, we are heading up to Jerusalem and the Son of Man will be handed over to the chief priests and the scribes and they will condemn him to death and hand him over to the gentiles ³⁴ and they will flog him and kill him and after three days he will rise."

³⁵ James and John, the sons of Zebedee, approached Jesus with a request, "Teacher, we want you to do us a favor." ³⁶ He responded, "What do you want me to do for you?" ³⁷ They said to him, "Grant us to sit at your right and left in your glory." ³⁸ Jesus responded, "You don't know what you're asking. Can you drink the cup that I drink or be baptized with the baptism with which I am being baptized?" ³⁹ They said, "Yes, we can." Jesus responded, "You can drink the cup I drink and be baptized with the baptism that I am being baptized with alright, ⁴⁰ but to sit on my right and left is not for me to give but is for whom it has been prepared."

⁴¹ Hearing all this, the ten began to be angry with James and John ⁴² and Jesus then summoned them together and said, "You know that those who think to be rulers of the gentiles lord it over them and their big people boss them around? ⁴³ It's not to be like that with you, but whoever wants to become great among you will be your servant ⁴⁴ and whoever wants to be first will be slave for all. ⁴⁵ For the Son of Man did not come to be served but to serve and to give his life a ransom for many."

⁴⁶ They reached Jericho. As he was leaving Jericho with his disciples and quite a crowd, the son of Timaeus, Bartimaeus, a blind beggar, who was sitting on the roadside, ⁴⁷ when he heard that it was Jesus of Nazareth, started calling out, "Son of David, have mercy on me!"

⁴⁸ Many told him off, to be quiet, but he cried out all the more, "Son of David, have mercy on me!" ⁴⁹ Jesus stopped and said, "Call

him." So they call the blind man, telling him, "Don't worry, get up, he's calling you." ⁵⁰ He dropped his garment, got up and went to Jesus. ⁵¹ Jesus responded to him, saying, "What do you want me to do for you?" The blind man replied, "*Rabbouni*, I want to be able to see!" ⁵² Jesus said to him, "Go, your faith has made you well."

And immediately his sight was restored, and he started following him on the way.

Thinking about Mark

For a third time, Mark reports Jesus' prediction that as Son of Man he would face suffering and death and then rise from the dead and immediately thereafter reports the disciples' getting it wrong (10:33–40, earlier 8:29–33; 9:30–34). Perhaps Mark means his hearers to make a connection between Jesus' resurrection and the thought of the coming kingdom. This might explain why James and John then decide to ask Jesus about the possibility of being given positions of power when it comes (10:35–37). Perhaps Mark means us also to consider what Jesus' resurrection really meant. Did it mean turning his back on lowliness and love and achieving what, after all, everyone might surely want, namely, glory and honor?

Mark presents the disciples as very fallible and as lacking insight, despite what he had said back in his section on parables about their being given secret knowledge (4:10–12). Peter's notion of messiahship had contradicted Jesus' way (8:29–31). Next Jesus finds his disciples arguing about who among them would be the greatest (9:34). Now, after announcing his path of suffering for a third time, James and John want places in glory and to be second in charge in the coming kingdom (10:35–37).

This deliberate depiction of the disciples' fallibility is very likely serving a purpose in Mark' day, namely, to warn disciples, and leaders in particular, against the folly of personal ambition, an agenda that remains relevant in every age. Matthew's twist to the story is perhaps unfairly to make the brothers' mother take the initiative (20:20), perhaps to protect their reputation but perhaps aware that sometimes family is not good news when it comes to ambition.

Mark has Jesus respond initially with a challenge to the brothers, asking whether they would they be prepared to be put through (be baptized in) suffering and drink its cup, to which they declare their willingness

(10:38–39). The passage through hardship to glory was a common theme in depicting heroes. Glory and power are what matters, even if you have to suffer on the way to reach it. Mark's hearers would have been familiar with the pattern. Jesus in any case steps back from the assumption that such leadership was his to give. Only God could do that.

Amid the anger of the other disciples about the brothers' move, Mark has Jesus engage in some sociological observation (10:41–42). He points out to them the way, at least in the gentile world, many who rule do so because they want to control and dominate. He speaks as a Jew to Jews and, of course, this malaise is not peculiar to gentiles—as the disciples have just illustrated.

Mark then has Jesus return to the message he had given them after he found them competing for status and had put before them the model of the small child not yet taken with the need to compete with others for status and acceptance (9:33–36). "Whoever wishes to become great among you must be your servant, and whoever wishes to be first among you must be slave of all" (10:43–44). This turns their ambitions upside down. The image of being a servant and a slave speaks not just of lowliness, and not of lowliness for its own sake, but lowliness in love. To be great is to be loving and caring.

It was not as though Jesus demanded this of his disciples while he looked forward to glory and power for himself. On the contrary, "the Son of Man did not come to be served but to serve" (10:45). Mark's story of Jesus has shown him doing just that, liberating people from their demons and bringing healing and hope to those around him. Jesus' words continue: "and to give his life a ransom for many" (10:45).

This is one of just two occasions where Mark has Jesus speak of his death as bringing benefit, a view that by Mark's time was integral to the message of the gospel. The other is at the last meal (14:24). Taken literally, paying a ransom was usually to set hostages free and was paid to those holding them captive. Does Mark really mean us to understand Jesus' death as paying God or perhaps Satan to set people free? This would be to fail to understand how such images worked and had been used in Jewish tradition. When, for instance, the scriptures spoke of God ransoming or redeeming Israel from Egypt (e.g., Pss 74:2; 77:15), it implied no such transaction, but simply meant liberation.

Very early in the movement one of the ways of coming to terms with Jesus' death was to see it not as a disaster and defeat, but as a victory of love and a source of grace and forgiveness. It summed up, in that sense, the liberating power that had been at work in Jesus' ministry and, inevitably for

THE IDENTITY

people in those times, it was like the way sacrifices were seen to bring good. Christ died for us, for our sins, was one of the simple ways of saying this.

Its mention here is significant because Mark is reaching the end of his depiction of Jesus' public ministry and has Jesus well on his way to Jerusalem where he would indeed lose his life. Mark does not portray Jesus as enduring such suffering and death primarily in order to be rewarded like a hero with glory, the price he had to pay to win the prize. Instead, he portrays Jesus as having a very different ambition: to follow through with his message and action to bring health and healing.

Nor does Mark indicate that this was a temporary task Jesus had to fulfill to reach his goal of glory. Rather, Mark depicts it as Jesus' way, integral to who he was. More than that, he indicates that in being like this, Jesus was reflecting God's priority and being. As he said to Peter, the first person to fail to understand his priorities, "You're focusing on human priorities not God's priorities" (8:33). Jesus' sociological observation applies just as much to people's image of God, which are often shaped by detail drawn from images of kings on glorious thrones wanting all to adore them.

Mark's story of Jesus' death reinforces the subversiveness of his message. Jesus is indeed a king, "the King of the Jews," but he is a king enthroned on a cross and crowned with a crown of thorns. This is not an interim stunt, an episode that must be reckoned as an exception in the life of God, as though God through Jesus chose temporally to be loving and then rewarded Jesus for putting on the act. Rather, Jesus, as the church would proclaim, reveals how and who God is.

As Mark had contrasted the disciples' failure to hear and see with Jesus' healings in 7:31-37 and 8:14-26, helping a deaf man to hear and a blind man to see, so the story of Jesus' healing of the blind man, Bartimaeus (8:16-21), may play a similar role, may indeed recall the earlier contrast. The disciples fail to see. Bartimaeus sees and declares Jesus to be "Son of David." At the story level, people around the blind beggar of Jericho try to silence him, but he persists. The truth will out. And Jesus is on his way, up from Jericho in the Jordan Valley to Jerusalem, where the rulers and authorities of his day will confront his claims for an alternative empire and kingdom based in love. They, too, will not see.

Reflection: In what ways did the disciples and Jesus have different understandings of what greatness meant: for themselves, for Jesus, and for God? How do you see these understandings expressing themselves today, in church, in worship, in politics, in daily life?

4

Jesus and the Temple

Grand Entry? (11:1–10)

Listening to Mark

11:1 When they were approaching Jerusalem and arrived at Bethphage and Bethany near the Mount of Olives, he sent off two of his disciples, **2** telling them, "Go into the hamlet opposite you and immediately as you enter it you will see a foal tied up that no one has yet ridden. Untie it and bring it. **3** And if anyone says, 'What are you doing,' say 'The master needs it, and he'll return it back here again.'" **4** And they went off and found the foal tied to the gate outside in the street and untied it. **5** And some standing there said to them, "What are you doing untying the foal?" **6** And they responded as Jesus had told them and they let them do it.

7 So they bring the foal to Jesus, and they threw their cloaks over it and he sat on it. **8** And many spread their garments on the road, and others cut branches from the fields **9** and both those going on ahead of him and those following him shouted, "Hosanna, blessed is the one who comes in the name of the Lord, **10** blessed is the coming kingdom of our father, David! Hosanna in the highest!"

Thinking about Mark

Finally, Jesus approaches Jerusalem and from across the valley on the Mount of Olives, a place where tradition envisaged resurrections from its tombs on the last day, Jesus prepares his entry. Good forward planning on his part? Or miraculous foreknowledge? Mark does not say, but the scene is set. A young donkey not yet ridden—an honor for Jesus, with more to come.

One might imagine the city coming to a standstill with all thronging to this major event. In our day TV cameras and journalists would lead the crush. Historically it is plausible that Jesus' entry was greeted by his admirers, but anything more than that, such as our fantasy might imagine, would have been quickly set upon by the Roman soldiers transferred there at Passover time to keep law and order when thousands made it to the city. More likely it was an event that attracted some and was over quickly enough not to draw too much attention.

Mark will not have been the first to tell these stories about Jesus' last days. We can imagine four decades of telling and retelling with much reflection before he came to write it down. Part of that process was to depict the events in the light of images drawn from biblical tradition. This is especially so in describing Jesus' crucifixion, where we see motifs drawn from the Psalms, especially Psalm 22.

We find it, however, already in earlier scenes. The prophecies of Zechariah have shaped storytellers' depictions. Zechariah 9:9 tells of Israel's king: "Rejoice greatly, O daughter Zion! Shout aloud, O daughter Jerusalem! Lo, your king comes to you; triumphant and victorious is he, humble and riding on a donkey, on a colt, the foal of a donkey." Matthew recognizes what in Mark is an allusion and cites it in full, somewhat awkwardly having Jesus fulfill the prediction by riding simultaneously on both animals ("he sat on *them*" 21:7; italics added)!

Allusions to Zechariah's visions of future hope also include the motifs: "the blood of my covenant" (9:11), perhaps alluded to in Mark's account of Jesus' last meal, and Zechariah 13:7 ("Strike the shepherd, that the sheep may be scattered"), cited immediately after (14:27). Zechariah's vision also influenced later retellings of Jesus' last days; the thirty shekels of silver, thrown into the treasury (11:12–13), reflected in Matthew's expansion of the story of Judas (26:15; 27:3–5) and John's citation of 12:10 ("when they look on the one whom they have pierced") in 19:37.

The citations above belong among Zechariah's predictions that envisage the king as a warrior and Israel as triumphant over the nations. The hopes do not match who Jesus was, but the expectation that in Jesus there would be fulfillment of Israel's hopes, even if quite differently, encouraged people to use such motifs. Hence the image of the king in lowliness riding on a donkey, a fitting image for Jesus as Mark portrays him, though not as having been "triumphant and victorious" in battle. It is therefore a misnomer to call Jesus' entry his *"triumphant* entry" unless accompanied with heavy qualifications.

Jesus rides into Jerusalem, according to Mark's story, to the acclamation of his followers. It was potentially dangerous but not big enough to warrant intervention. The crowd's acclamation: "Hosanna! Blessed is the one who comes in the name of the Lord! Blessed is the coming kingdom of our father, David! Hosanna in the highest!" (11:9-10) is drawn in part from Psalm 118, "Blessed is the one who comes in the name of the Lord" (118:26), an acclamation of those approaching Jerusalem, which speaks of a "festal procession with branches" (118:27), and from Psalm 148, "Praise him [represented in Mark by 'Hosanna'] in the heights" (148:1).

Mark or his tradition has supplemented it with the words: "Blessed is the coming kingdom of our father, David!" (11:10). This implies that the crowd is acclaiming Jesus the Messiah, the hoped for Son of David, the title with which Bartimaeus had shortly before hailed Jesus (10:47-48). This coheres with the image of Jesus coming as king in the allusion to Zechariah 9. In John's Gospel we read, "His disciples did not understand these things at first; but when Jesus was glorified, then they remembered that these things had been written of him and had been done to him" (12:16). This is a puzzling statement, especially since it had just had Jesus hailed by the crowd as "the king of Israel" and cited the Zechariah passage.

Did the crowd really hail him as Messiah and the disciples not understand this till later? Perhaps the original event had no such messianic overtones, which were then derived from a storyteller creating or recreating the scene, based on Zechariah 9. Was there such a grand entry at all or was it imagined on the basis of Zechariah? There is no reference back to it in Mark's story, unlike with Jesus' actions in the temple. We cannot know for sure. In Mark's storyline, it fits the theme of Jesus hailed as Son of David and approaching Jerusalem as its Messiah, but as a very different Messiah from what popular expectation envisaged.

There was however a widespread expectation that the coming of the Messiah would bring about the restoration of the temple. Indeed, it was the first celebrated "Son of David"—namely David's son, Solomon, who succeeded him on the throne—who erected it. When Herod the Great undertook a major rebuilding of the temple, one may suspect that he might have been seeking to give the impression that he was the ideal king to whom people should look. These two themes, Jesus as Messiah and Jesus and the temple's future, underlie Mark's story in the following chapters. They come to a climax at Jesus' Jewish trial where the two themes are central.

Reflection: Was it a "grand entry" or what was it? Did Jesus court popularity and seek adulation? How might you imagine yourself in the crowd?

Jesus and the Temple Establishment (11:11–26)

Listening to Mark

¹¹ So he entered Jerusalem and went straight into the temple, and he was looking around at it all, but because it was already evening, he left again for Bethany with the twelve. ¹² The next day on their way out of Bethany he was hungry ¹³ and seeing a fig tree in leaf in the distance went to see if he could find any fruit on it and when he got there he found none, just leaves because it wasn't yet the season for fruit. ¹⁴ In response he said to it, "Never again may anyone eat fruit from you!" And his disciples heard him.
¹⁵ So they came into Jerusalem and entering the temple, he began to drive out those who were engaged in selling and buying things in the temple and he upturned the tables of the moneychangers and the seats of those selling doves ¹⁶ and would not allow people to carry anything through the temple. ¹⁷ And he was teaching and said to them, "Is it not written that 'My house shall be called a house of prayer for all peoples'? But you have turned it into a den of robbers." ¹⁸ Now the chief priests and the scribes heard about this and looked for a way that they could do away with him, but they had their fears about him, because the crowd was quite taken by his teaching. ¹⁹ When evening came, they left for outside the city.
²⁰ As they were going along early next morning, they saw that the fig tree had withered. ²¹ Peter remembered and says to him, "Rabbi, look! The fig tree that you cursed has withered." ²² Jesus responded, "Have faith in God. ²³ Truly I tell you whoever says to this mountain, 'Get uprooted and thrown into the sea' and does not doubt in their mind but has faith, that they say will happen, it will indeed happen for them. ²⁴ That's why I am telling you, everything you pray about and ask for, have faith that you will get it, and you will indeed get it. ²⁵ And when you stand praying, be forgiving if you have something against someone, so that your Father in heaven may also forgive you your wrongdoings."

JESUS AND THE TEMPLE

Thinking about Mark

It is not insignificant that Mark has Jesus first visit the temple. Mark tells us no more than that Jesus "looked around at everything" (11:11) and then exited the city to stay overnight in Bethany nearby with his disciples. Why even mention the visit after such an entry? In part, it is because an important aspect of being the Messiah was to be concerned about the temple. Mark probably also wants us to know that when Jesus would go on the next day to make judgments about the temple, he did so on an informed basis.

In describing what happened next, Mark employs symbolism using his familiar sandwich technique of interpreting one story by placing it within another. At a literal level he has Jesus feel hungry, look at a fig tree for a fig to eat, find none, and then curse it (11:12–14), a seemingly rather petulant act until we see what Mark is doing. He is having Jesus pass judgment on the temple—or better the temple authorities—for failing to bear the fruit of justice and goodness. By the next day the tree had withered as if by magic (11:20–21), but Mark would understand it as the result of Jesus' condemnation.

In between the cursing of the fig tree and its withering is the event it symbolizes: Jesus' demonstration that the temple (regime) is to be condemned (11:15–19). He drives out those selling animals for sacrifice and overturns the tables of those managing the currency exchange necessary to enable people to donate in Tyrian shekels, as was required, and he stops people carrying things through the temple. Why? His words, "Is it not written, 'My house shall be called a house of prayer for all peoples'? But you have turned it into a den of robbers'" (11:17), might sound like he is accusing sellers and buyers of overcharging, and was in that sense "cleansing" the temple, but that is unlikely.

Mark has Jesus do much more than suggest exploitation by those meant to resource worshippers. He is not about improving the temple, nor about uncluttering the outer court from such activities, so as to make more room for foreigners. For Mark will go on to have Jesus condemn temple authorities for exploiting widows and much more in his exchanges with them (11:27—12:37). He will announce the temple's destruction and replacement by another not made with hands, namely the faith community he had initiated. His first actions in the temple are therefore best understood as symbolic acts representing what he saw as God's judgment against the institution, typical of prophetic symbolic acts in Israel's traditions.

The shriveled fig tree declares the temple's fate. Mark's hearers may well have been very aware that close to their time in 70 CE the Romans had destroyed the temple as part of crushing the revolt that broke out already in 66 CE and took another three years to bring to an end. The Greek word behind the common translation "robbers," in "den of robbers," was also the word for brigands. Mark and his hearers may have been aware that some revolutionary groups had made the temple their base during the revolt.

In Mark's account Jesus cites Isaiah 56:7 ("My house shall be called a house of prayer for all peoples"), which looks to a day when gentiles would come and sacrifice in the temple, and also Jeremiah 7:11, which charges temple authorities with turning the temple into a "den of robbers." The Isaiah quotation would have reminded Mark's hearers of the way the gospel had now reached the gentile nations, including the nations of which they themselves were a part. Jeremiah's judgment was one of many instances where prophets and others attacked the temple personnel, including sometimes predicting that the outcome would be the temple's destruction.

Mark's version of the story seems closely entwined with his emphasis on the inclusion of the gentiles and the church as replacing the temple. This may reflect a way of interpreting the event closer to Mark's time or at least at a time when the mission to the gentiles had developed. It is difficult therefore to reconstruct what might have been the emphases in earlier forms of the story. A consistent element, however, appears to have been the charge of abuse and the prediction that this abuse would bring judgment. This element probably goes right back to Jesus. John's Gospel, which less convincingly relocates the event to the beginning of Jesus' ministry, nevertheless also reflects this primary focus on confronting abuse rather than on saying something about gentiles. It, too, however, knows the tradition about Jesus' speaking of a new temple, interpreting it in its own way as referring to his resurrected body.

There seems, therefore, little doubt that Jesus performed a symbolic prophetic act in the outer court of the temple in order to confront the temple system and its minders. The outer court, however, was a huge area, the size of six football fields and would have been filled with thousands of people. It hardly makes sense, therefore, to claim that Jesus engaged in the massive undertaking of clearing it, which would have taken hours and would have brought intervention of Roman soldiers with overview of the court from their adjacent tower. A symbolic act did not require such a major undertaking.

Rather we are best to imagine that in one corner of this outer court teeming with people, Jesus performed his act and could then just as quickly disappear to safety in the crowd. To be effective it would have to be seen and known, but not to the extent that the authorities could intervene. Both Mark's and John's account suggest that Jesus must have said something in association with it about the temple's destruction and its replacement within a short time, proverbially expressed as "after three days." John has Jesus declare in the context of his symbolic act: "Destroy this temple, and in three days I will raise it up" (2:19) and Mark reports the charge brought against Jesus at his Jewish trial, likely to be a perversion of what he actually said: "We heard him say, 'I shall destroy this temple made with hands and in three days build another one not made with hands'" (14:58). The false component in the saying is the allegation that he himself would destroy the temple.

Mark's view of the temple theme becomes clear when we observe what he was doing in employing his sandwich technique: the temple authorities have not borne the fruit of justice and so the tree has shriveled. The temple is doomed. Mark will echo his depiction of Jesus' prediction of the temple's destruction when he has Jesus make it explicit in Mark 13.

In between the cursing of the fig tree and the explicit prediction of the temple's demise in chapter 13, Mark helps his hearers further understand why and how it would be replaced. Its replacement will also be reflected in Mark's conclusion of the parable of the vineyard, which cites Psalm 118 again, that the stone the builders rejected has become the chief cornerstone (118:22). It is also reflected in Jesus' saying that there is to be a temple not made with hands (14:58). Jesus is the foundation of the new temple, which comprises people.

Mark's connecting Peter's discovery of the withered fig tree with statements about faith and prayer (11:20–25) may already be pointing to the community of the disciples as a place of prayer replacing the temple, which was meant to be a house of prayer for all nations. The connection is rather loose, though "this mountain" would be referring to the temple mount. Mark is having Jesus assert that faith can do extraordinary things.

The notion that they will also get what they want appears wonderfully exaggerated: moving mountains! It falls flat on its face, however, in the hands of those who then want to use prayer to serve their greed. Faith is not about moving mountains literally, but it does enable people to deal with obstacles set in the path of the gospel. By adding the exhortation about forgiveness (11:25) Mark has Jesus identify one of the obstacles that can be found right in the heart of faith communities and can make also its structures crumble.

Reflection: What was Jesus saying by his action in the temple and what does Mark see it foreshadowing? What now replaces the temple, according to Mark? Can what went wrong then also go wrong now?

Confrontations (11:27—12:44)

Listening to Mark

⁷²⁷ And they went again into Jerusalem and were walking around in the temple when the chief priests and the scribes and the elders came ²⁸ and confronted him saying, "By what authority are you doing these things or who gave you this authority for doing them?" ²⁹ Jesus replied to them, "Let me ask you a questions and if you answer me, I will then tell you by what authority I am doing these things. ³⁰ The baptism of John, was it from heaven or just a human initiative? Answer me!" ³¹ They discussed it among themselves along the lines that if we say from heaven, he will say then why didn't you believe me ³² and if we say just human, they feared the crowd, because they all held John to be a prophet. ³³ So in response to Jesus, they say, "We don't know." So Jesus says to them, "Then neither will I tell you by what authority I am doing these things."

¹²:¹ And he began to speak to them in parables. "A man planted a vineyard, put a fence around it, dug a winepress, built a tower, and leased it to tenants and went off on a journey. ² So he sent a slave to the tenants at the appropriate time to get some of the grape harvest from the tenants, ³ but they grabbed him and beat him up and sent him off empty. ⁴ And again, he sent another slave to them and that man they bashed and humiliated. ⁵ He then sent another and that one they killed, and many others, some of whom they beat up and others they killed. ⁶ He still had one more option, his beloved son. He sent him last of all to them, thinking they will surely respect my son. ⁷ But those tenants said to one another, 'He's the heir. Come on, let's kill him and the inheritance will be ours.' ⁸ And grabbing him, they killed him and threw him out of the vineyard. ⁹ What will the master of the vineyard do? He will come and destroy those tenants and give the vineyard to others. ¹⁰ Have you not read the scripture, 'The stone which the builders rejected had become the cornerstone; ¹¹ this is the Lord's doing and it is marvelous in our eyes'?" ¹² They sought to arrest him but feared

the crowd, for they knew that he had told the parable against them. So they left him and went away.

[13] Then they send some of the Pharisees and the Herodians to him to trip him up in discussion. [14] They came and asked him, "Teacher, we know that you are truthful, and you're not bothered by what anyone thinks, because you don't take people at face value, but have been genuinely teaching the way of God. Is it lawful to pay tax to the emperor or not? Do we pay or don't we?" [15] He recognized their hypocrisy and said to them, "Why are you putting me to the test? Bring me a denarius so that I can look at it." [16] They brought one and he said, "Whose image and inscription is this?" And they answered, "The emperor's." [17] Then Jesus said, "Give the emperor what is the emperor's and God what is God's." And they marveled at his response.

[18] Next some Sadducees, who say there's no resurrection from the dead, came to him, and they put a question to him: [19] "Teacher, Moses wrote that if anyone's brother dies and leaves a wife behind and has not had children, his brother should take her as his wife and generate offspring for his brother. [20] Now there were seven brothers. The first took a wife and died without producing offspring. [21] So the second brother took her, but he died, too, not leaving any offspring and the third, likewise. [22] All seven failed to produce offspring. And last of all the woman herself died. [23] Now at the resurrection who will have her as his wife, because all seven had had her as their wife?"

[24] Jesus said to them, "You're off track on this, not knowing the scripture nor the power of God. [25] For when they rise from the dead, they neither marry nor are given in marriage but are like the angels in heaven. [26] And as far as the dead being raised, haven't you read in the book of Moses in the burning bush episode, how God said to him, 'I am the God of Abraham and the God of Isaac and the God of Jacob'? [27] God is not God of the dead but of the living. You are well off track!"

[28] One of the scribes who heard their discussion came and said to him, "You answered that well." And he asked him, "What is the first commandment of all?" [29] Jesus replied, "The first is 'Hear, O Israel, the Lord your God, the Lord is one. [30] And you shall love the Lord your God with all your heart, and with all your soul, and with all your mind and with all your strength.' [31] And the second is this: 'You shall love your neighbor as yourself.' There is no other commandment greater than these." [32] And the scribe said to him, "Yes. Teacher, you have

spoken truly, because 'There is one and beside him is no other' [33] and 'to love him from all one's heart and all one's understanding and all one's strength' and 'to love one's neighbor as oneself,' is more important than all burnt offerings and sacrifices." [34] And Jesus, recognizing that he had answered wisely, responded, "You are not far from the kingdom of God." And no one dared to ask him any more.

[35] Having replied, Jesus went on teaching in the temple and posed the question, "How come the scribes say that the Messiah is the Son of David? [36] Didn't David, himself, inspired by the Holy Spirit, say, 'The Lord said to my master, "Sit at my right hand until I make your enemies a footstool for your feet"'? [37] So if David calls him his master, how could he be his son?" The crowd listened to him gladly.

[38] In his teaching he declared, "Beware of the scribes who like to walk about in robes and be greeted in the marketplaces [39] and take the best seats in the synagogues and the top positions in feasts, [40] who also devour the households of widows and make long prayers just for show. They will face all the greater condemnation."

[41] And he was sitting opposite the treasury watching how people put money into the treasury. And many rich people put in a lot. [42] Then a poor widow came along, and she put in two lepta, worth a quadrant. [43] Summoning his disciples, he told them. "Truly I tell you this poor widow has put in more than all those who have been putting money into the treasury. [44] They have all been donating from their surplus, but she has done so out of her poverty, giving everything she had, her whole livelihood."

Thinking about Mark

Mark does not report that "the chief priests, the scribes, and the elders" were immediately on the scene to challenge what Jesus did in the temple. Instead, he indicates that at least a day or two passed before they confronted Jesus and then the issue was his authority (11:27–33). Authority had been an issue with John the Baptist because of his novel initiative to offer God's forgiveness to all on repentance, symbolized by his immersing them in the Jordan.

It was not that they would have disputed that God is forgiving, but rather their concern was that John was operating outside what were the divinely mandated structures of the temple and its priests. They could not deny that there was some good in what he did, and that people flocked to him for baptism, probably including some of them. Therefore, when Jesus asserts that his authority is similar, they are stymied and refuse to be drawn on John's authority.

Mark then has Jesus go on to challenge them through a very pointed parable about tenants of a vineyard who fail in their task (12:1–9). In the biblical tradition, the prophet Isaiah had spoken of Israel as like a vineyard (5:1–7) and the image was current. Here the focus of the parable is not the vines themselves, but those meant to look after them. It may go back to a parable Jesus told, but in its present form it has been very much shaped in the light of later Christian reflection. Maltreating and killing the slaves alludes to how Israel's leaders treated many of the prophets, and killing the son obviously alludes to Jesus' crucifixion.

When Mark has Jesus end the parable with the words, "What will the master of the vineyard do? He will come and destroy those tenants and give the vineyard to others" (12:9), he is clearly referring to the temple's demise, and thereby the demise of the temple authorities. There is even more: they are to be replaced by new authorities, namely, as we are to infer, the leaders of the Jesus movement. The reference to destruction may well be Mark's reflection on the sacking of Jerusalem and the destruction of the temple by the Romans in 70 CE. The people of God, represented as the vineyard, are now under new leadership.

Matthew makes very explicit his view that 70 CE was God's act of judgment against Jerusalem and its people for rejecting Jesus and the messengers of the Jesus movement. Attributing that terrible event—accompanied by slaughter of men, women, and children—to God goes beyond what a theology of justice and compassion can tolerate and reflects the fallibility in a movement concerned to defend itself and deal with the pain and anger of rejection.

Mark has Jesus explicate the implications of the parable by citing Psalm 118:22 as applicable to Jesus, the Son: "The stone that the builders rejected has become the cornerstone; this is the Lord's doing and it is marvelous in our eyes" (12:10–11). If an earlier form of the story was told in Hebrew, its hearers would have noticed the play on words between "stone" *eben* and "son" *ben*. In Mark's storyline the authorities are in no doubt that the parable was targeting them, but held off making an arrest, given his popularity.

Mark had already referred twice to the alliance of the Pharisees and the Herodians, presumably the personnel serving Herod Antipas (3:6; 8:15). Their trick question in 12:13–17 is deliberately wanting to get Jesus into trouble. His answer is equally tricky: give to God what is God's and to the emperor what is the emperor's, but of course all is God's! So Jesus neither sides with the anti-imperial forces nor does he surrender to submission to Rome.

The next question comes from the Sadducees (12:18–27), another group with influence, especially in the Jerusalem administration in Jesus' time. It was characterized by resistance to innovative ideas, such as resurrection from the dead and immortality of the soul, and instead held to what Jews had traditionally believed for centuries and what is generally reflected in the Hebrew Bible. Their question is designed to make such innovative beliefs look ridiculous. Is the poor woman going to be simultaneously married to seven husbands in your idea of a resurrection? Absurd!

The response Mark has Jesus give meets the issue raised by declaring that there would be no marriage in the age to come. This is not suggesting there would be sexual freedom and approved promiscuity, nor is it just about weddings. It reflects rather the belief that resurrection life would not be simply a repeat of ordinary physical life. Images of resurrection tend to picture a kind of spiritual embodiment, such as we see in stories of Jesus after his resurrection, where he is seen to appear and disappear. Paul talks of resurrection bodies as being spiritual, not physical, bodies (1 Cor 15:42–44). In addition, there was the view that the age to come would mean entering sacred space, where in any case sexual relations were forbidden.

The argument based on references to God as the God of Abraham, Isaac, and Jacob assumes that such references imply that they were still alive or would be alive at the resurrection, which is not, of course, what the references originally meant. Mark had Jesus begin his response with reference to what is possible for God. No real answer is given beyond the explanation that resurrection life will be of a kind where issues such as sex and marriage will no longer have relevance. Luke has Jesus supplement the answer by suggesting that if they are to be like angels and have everlasting life, then they do not need to reproduce and for that reason alone sex becomes irrelevant. His addition reflects a narrow view current in some circles of the time that sexual intercourse has and should have only a reproductive role.

The next dispute (12:28–34) is relatively irenic, indeed, hardly a dispute because it ends with Mark having Jesus declare that the scribe who had questioned him was "not far from the kingdom of God" (12:34), but not there yet. They are very close in sharing what was good Judaism, namely that loving God and one's neighbor has a higher priority "than all whole burnt-offerings and sacrifices" (12:33). The prophets and psalmists had made the same point (e.g., Ps 40:6; Hos 6:6). Matthew twice inserts a reference to Hosea 6:6 ("I desire mercy, not sacrifice") into accounts of Jesus' disputes with fellow Jews (9:13; 12:7).

Such a perspective would have helped Jews living far from the temple, and especially those living after its destruction, to come to terms with having to live without the temple and its sacrifices. It never meant rejection of sacrifices. It was a matter of priority. In Mark it is likely that it does imply rejection of sacrifices, just as Mark uses Jesus' saying about what makes a person unclean in 7:15 to reject biblical teaching about unclean foods, taking it beyond its likely original meaning, which was a comment about priorities.

The scribe was not far from the kingdom of God. To join it, as Mark would see it, would be to embrace the claims of Jesus about himself and see that he replaces the temple. While Matthew affirms the contrast, as shown by his insertions of Hosea 6:6 earlier, he omits both the reference to the scribe's comments about sacrifices when he repeats Mark's story and deletes the half-commendation that the scribe was not far from the kingdom of God. Instead, he has Jesus declare that the Law and the Prophets, which for him remain totally in force (5:18–19), hang on these two great commandments. Similarly, Luke similarly trims the episode, repurposing and relocating it earlier in his story, to make it his introduction to the parable of good Samaritan (10:25–28) and have it introduced with the question that Mark's rich man asked: "What must I do to inherit eternal life?" (10:25).

Having concluded that Jesus' answers to their questions had silenced his critics, Mark has Jesus address the issue of his identity, challenging the adequacy of "Son of David" as a designation of the Messiah (12:35–37). This seems more likely to be an issue in Mark's day where much more was being claimed of Jesus than that he was the Messiah of the Jews. The "proof" cited to refute it, Psalm 110:1, is one of the major texts used in the movement to interpret Jesus' resurrection, namely as God's enthroning Jesus at his right hand as the Messiah. "The LORD says to my master, 'Sit at my right hand until I make your enemies your footstool.'" Its introduction, "The LORD said to my master," reports a psalmist's acclamation of a king's enthronement, speaking of the psalmist's master.

Where, however, the popular assumption was that David wrote the Psalms, the argument might work that the one being enthroned must be David's superior and where it was understood to refer to the Messiah to come and to Jesus as the Messiah, then a higher status for Jesus as Messiah is to be assumed than "Son of David" suggests. "Son of God," like "Son of David," was a title used of kings and so of the royal Messiah to come and therefore of Jesus, but clearly Mark wants to say that, being God's Son, Jesus was much more than a Davidic king. He had a special relationship with God, who both addressed him at his baptism and acclaimed him before others on the mountain as "My Son" (1:11; 9:7).

Mark offers us little to fill out this special status, nothing about existence from the beginning of creation as in John 1:1, nor anything about a miraculous conception, as in Matthew and Luke, nor anything like later doctrines of the Trinity, but certainly a status not just reached by his resurrection, but also affirmed at least from his baptism. Mark wants his hearers to see this. To take this step would take the scribe into the kingdom of God.

Mark's final episode (12:38–40) recounts Jesus' earlier words of judgment against the temple establishment. Mark portrays Jesus as confronting scribes who seem bent of self-aggrandizement while exploiting the vulnerable, especially poor widows. By contrast, Mark has Jesus point to one such widow's sacrificial giving (12:41–44). At this point in following Mark's story, Matthew replaces Mark's brief confrontation and the hailing of the widow with a whole lengthy chapter enumerating the abuses of scribes and Pharisees (23:1–39). Many will be abuses from Matthew's own time when, in the decades following the destruction of the temple in 70 CE and the demise of the Sadducean party, the Pharisees and their scribes had assumed leadership of a resurgent Judaism. Mark's brief account, nevertheless, sets the scene for the prediction of the temple's destruction in the following chapter, seen as a judgment not of a building but of its leaders and of their corrupt practices.

Reflection: What priorities does Mark have Jesus set? Why is the scribe described as not far from the kingdom of God? What steps are missing? To what extent do the challenges Jesus faced also play a role today?

Predicting the Temple's Destruction and History's Climax (13:1–37)

Listening to Mark

^{13:1} On the way out of the temple, one of his disciples says to him, "Teacher, wow! Look at those great stone blocks and those buildings!" ² And Jesus said to him, "You see these great buildings? Not one stone block will be left on another here that won't be toppled."

³ And while they were sitting on the Mount of Olives opposite the temple, Peter and James and John were asking him privately, ⁴ "Tell us, when will these things happen and what will be the indication that all these things are going to come to their end?" ⁵ Jesus started telling them, "Beware that no one leads you astray. ⁶ Because many will come in my name saying, 'I'm him' and will lead many astray. ⁷ When you hear of wars and rumors of wars, don't panic; it has to be, but that won't yet be the end. ⁸ For nation will rise up against nation and kingdom against kingdom and there will be earthquakes in various places and famines; that's just the start of the birth pangs.

⁹ Watch out, because they will hand you over to tribunals and give you a beating in their synagogues and bring you before governors and emperors for my sake to testify before them. ¹⁰ But first the good news story must be proclaimed to every nation. ¹¹ And when they arraign you before authorities, don't worry about what you should say, because you'll say what is given you at that time, because it is not you speaking, but the Holy Spirit. ¹² Brother will betray brother to death and fathers, sons, and children will turn against their parents and have them killed. ¹³ And you will be hated by everyone for my sake, but whoever holds out to the end will be saved.

¹⁴ When you see the desolating sacrilege set up where it should not be—let the reader understand—then those in Judea should flee to the hills. ¹⁵ If someone's up on their roof, they shouldn't come down and go to fetch things from their house ¹⁶ and if someone's out on land, they shouldn't go back to fetch their clothes. ¹⁷ And pity the woman who is pregnant or breastfeeding in those days. ¹⁸ Pray that it doesn't

happen in winter. ¹⁹ Those days will have affliction such as has never been since the beginning of creation which God brought into being until now, the present time. ²⁰ And had not the Lord shortened those days, no human flesh would survive, but for the sake of the elect whom he has chosen, he shortened those days.

²¹ And then if anyone says, 'Here is the Messiah or look, there he is,' don't believe them. ²² For false Messiahs will arise and false prophets and they will perform signs and wonders in order to try, if possible, to lead astray even the elect. ²³ Watch out! I've told you all this in advance. ²⁴ But in those days after that affliction, 'the sun will be darkened, and the moon cease to shine, ²⁵ and the stars will start falling' from heaven and the powers in the heavens will be shaken. ²⁶ And then they will see the Son of Man coming on the clouds with great power and glory ²⁷ and then he will send his angels out and gather the elect from the four winds from the ends of the earth to the ends of heaven.

²⁸ Learn from what happens with the fig tree. When its branch is still developing and starts to produce leaves, you know that the harvest is not far away. ²⁹ So it will be with you. When you see these things happening, you know that it is close, right near your gates. ³⁰ Truly I tell you, this generation will not pass away before all these things take place. ³¹ Heaven and earth shall pass away, but my words shall not pass away.

³² But about the timing of that day and hour no one knows, neither the angels in heaven nor the Son, but only the Father. ³³ Watch out, keep awake! Because you don't know when the moment will arrive. ³⁴ It's like when a man sets off on a trip leaving his household behind and putting his slaves in charge, assigning a task to each and telling the doorkeeper to stay alert. ³⁵ Stay alert, then! For you don't know when the master of the household will return, whether late or in the middle of the night or at cock crows or early morning, ³⁶ lest he suddenly arrive and find you sleeping. ³⁷ What I'm telling you, I'm telling everyone: Be alert!"

Thinking about Mark

Mark began his depiction of Jesus' Jerusalem visit with Jesus' entry into the temple to look around (11:11). Now he completes the cycle, showing

Jesus leaving the temple after another visit (13:1). Perhaps Mark means something symbolic in describing his exit. In between Jesus had come and gone. He had caused a fig tree to shrivel, foreshadowing the temple establishment's demise because it failed to bear the fruit of justice and goodness. He had performed a prophetic act in the outer court, symbolizing judgment against the temple establishment as a house of exploiters, had engaged a range of fellow Jewish groups associated with the establishment, and had included a reference to the founding of a new temple with himself as the chief cornerstone. He had ended his final visit with another challenge of exploitation. The temple and its establishment will have to go. Now he abandons it.

The disciples wonder on the way out at the large stones and buildings of what was seen at the time as one of the Empire's most magnificent buildings (13:1–2). For Mark's hearers this detail might have brought to mind Jesus' citation of Psalm 118:22 a short time earlier, that the stone that the builders rejected would become the chief cornerstone. By contrast, these massive stones are to be overturned, the temple building destroyed. For Mark's hearers it was relatively recent history and still today one can see the massive stones that formed the platform on which Herod the Great had undertaken the temple's reconstruction over at least forty-six years, as John's Gospel tells us (2:20).

Having withdrawn across the valley to the Mount of Olives—a place of cemetery and of expectation of end events, including resurrections—Jesus engages in a private conversation with the inner group of his disciples, Peter, James, and John (13:3–4). They had been privy to the vision of his future end-time splendor on the mountain in Galilee (9:1–8). Now they want to know when the temple's destruction will occur and what signs they should look for that will indicate it is near. Mark's hearers would have been able to offer an informed answer in retrospect.

We may imagine they would nod their heads in agreement as Mark has Jesus describe phenomena that in their lifetime they had seen (13:5–8). This included the reference to would-be Messiahs, militia figures, prominent in the revolt of 66–70 CE, leading insurgencies. Mark has Jesus then go beyond 70 CE to address what might potentially face hearers of the gospel well after 70 CE. Reference to wars between nations, natural disasters, earthquakes, and famines were standard expectations in predictions of what the future might hold. They are not the end of the world. They precede it.

The predictions of persecution, whether through Jewish synagogues or at the hands of civil authorities, and of alienation and conflict in families (13:9–13), reflect what some of Mark's hearers will have already faced, as does the reference to expansion of the movement out into the world of gentile nations. When Mark's Jesus alludes to the sacrilege in the temple (13:14–23), originally describing what Antiochus IV Epiphanes set up in the temple in 167 BCE (Dan 11:31; 12:11), it may well have evoked memory of the highly offensive act planned by Roman Emperor Caligula in the 40s CE, to set up his legions' standards (which depicted animals, idolatrous images) or perhaps even a statue of himself, in the temple.

Mark may well be wanting his hearers to see a reference to more recent events ("let the reader understand" 13:14), when Jerusalem's believers had to flee to safety in Pella across the Jordan as Roman encirclement began, as the historian Eusebius, writing two centuries later, reports. Disaster and deception await them (13:14–23). The predictions are vague but dour. Mark has Jesus comfort his hearers that it will not go on for long (13:20). There will be hope.

When? In this generation, according to Mark: "this generation will not pass away before all these things have taken place" (13:30), echoing the prediction in 9:1 that the kingdom would come during the lifetime of some standing there. "All these things" also include what Mark has Jesus just enumerate, including events in the heavens, involving sun, moon, and stars, and his own return as Son of Man with his angels who will gather the elect from all four corners of the earth (13:24–27). They should look for the signs just as they look for signs of ripening of figs on a fig tree (13:28–29).

For Mark and his hearers, all the signs apparently pointed to history's climax, but the exact timing, Mark has Jesus assure them, not even Jesus, himself, knew (13:32). Just be ready! Watch! This, at least, kept guesswork at bay for them. For us, the timing is clearly not accurate. It did not happen within their generation, and it has not happened in the nearly two thousand years since. Twisting and turning the text to make it say something else is no more needed than to peddle a fantasy that they did not really believe the earth is flat.

Failure of such predictions to come true would have threatened to discredit the faith if such predictions were its center. They were not, and faith and its deep meaning in love remained and remains, despite our having major differences from the first followers of Jesus in the way we understand both space and time. This is equally the case with Paul, who expected to be alive when Christ returned to gather his own (1 Thess 4:15). Mark reflects the same notion of gathering, reflecting the assumption that most would still be alive (13:27). Paul supplements this with the information that those who had died would be raised to join them.

If Mark connects the destruction of the temple in 70 CE to the events leading up to history's end, Matthew, writing perhaps a decade and a half later, keeps them apart when he rewrites this section of Mark. Instead of having the disciples ask when the temple would be destroyed, he has them ask: "Tell us, when will this be, and what will be the sign of your coming and of the end of the age?" (24:3), two separate questions, moving the focus from the temple's destruction to the broader issue of Jesus' coming and the end of the age. Matthew then also omits the saying, "This generation will not pass away until all these things have taken place" (Mark 13:30), though he retains the saying of Mark 9:1 in Matt 16:28.

Luke leaves the question largely intact (21:7), but has the future predictions made while Jesus is teaching the people in the temple. He has Jesus speak of a time following the temple's destruction during which the city would be trampled by gentiles before their time is up and finally the end comes (21:24). Then Jerusalem's inhabitants, so long downtrodden, should lift up their eyes to see the coming of their Messiah (21:28), for Luke envisages that Jesus would return to reign from Jerusalem. Both Matthew and Luke, therefore, make a clear distinction between what happened a decade or two before their time, the destruction of the temple in 70 CE, and events predicted to take place before Jesus' return and the end of history.

Mark 13 has special character. It belongs to a pattern where authors seek to imagine what a hero's final advice might be for coming generations of followers, especially of the author's own generation. Often, they expand upon historical sayings or sayings passed down through tradition, but they go far beyond that. The book of Deuteronomy presents itself as Moses' last words. In Mark's day there had been many writings devoted entirely to such advice. They were called "Testaments." There was a Testament of Moses, a Testament of Abraham, and a Testament of the Twelve Patriarchs. All seek to imagine what their heroes would want to say to future generations, especially their own. All four canonical gospel writers engage this strategy.

Matthew takes over Mark's final main speech of Jesus to his select disciples with just a few modifications (24:1–51). They include distinguishing between the prediction of the temple's destruction and the prediction about the end of time, but also having Jesus express concern that when the believers in Jerusalem would have to flee, it would not only not be in winter but also not be on the Sabbath lest they breach Sabbath law (24:20), reflecting Matthew's strong commitment to keeping the law. He then adds another whole chapter in which Jesus spells out what people should be doing in the meantime, which the three parables of the young virgins, the talents, and the sheep and goats makes abundantly plain (25:1–46).

Luke keeps Mark 13 intact but now portrays it as public teaching in the temple (21:5–38). Instead, he creates a new composition of Jesus' final advice to his disciples, placing it in the context of their last meal together. He creates it by bringing together some traditions about Jesus' teaching from earlier, including material he found in Mark 10 (22:24–38). The author of John's Gospel goes much further, putting together a lengthy address from Jesus to his disciples, which extends over four chapters 13:31—16:33, with signs that it had been expanded over the years, with an appendix in the form of a prayer in John 17. These final words of Jesus to his own are characterized by warning and encouragement as disciples in future face challenges.

Reflection: To what extent do you see Mark's account of Jesus' final address reflecting issues of his day? What would you take from this address as relevant for our time? How might you imagine Jesus offering such last words of wisdom to us today?

… 5 …

The End?

Jesus Facing the End (14:1–21)

Listening to Mark

14:1 Passover was in two days' time and the festival of Unleavened Bread, and the chief priests and scribes were looking for a way to seize him by stealth and put him to death. **2** For they were saying that it couldn't be at the festival, because the people would be up in arms.

3 When he was in Bethany in the house of Simon the leper and was reclining at table, a woman came with an alabaster box containing some expensive oil of nard. She broke the container open and poured it on his head. **4** Some who were present shared together their feelings of anger, "Why this waste of myrrh? **5** This myrrh could have been sold for over three hundred denarii and the proceeds given to the poor." So they told her off. **6** But Jesus said to them, "Leave her be! Why hassle her? She's done something nice to me. **7** You'll always have the poor with you, and you can help them any time you want, but you won't always have me. **8** She's done what she could. She's anointed my body in advance for my burial. **9** I tell you, wherever the good news story is proclaimed in all the world, what she has done will be talked about in her memory."

10 Now Judas Iscariot, one of the twelve, went to the chief priests offering to hand him over to them. **11** Hearing this they were pleased and promised to give him money. So he sought an appropriate opportunity to betray him.

[12] On the first day of Unleavened Bread, when Passover is celebrated, his disciples say to him, "Where do you want us to go to prepare to eat the Passover?" [13] So he sends two of his disciples off, telling them, "Go into the city and a man will meet you carrying a pitcher of water. Follow him [14] and where he goes in, say to the householder that the teacher was asking, 'Where is the guest room where I can eat Passover with my disciples?' [15] And he will show you a big furnished room all ready, so make preparations for us there." [16] So the disciples set off and went into the city and found it just like he said and made preparation for Passover.

[17] In the evening he comes with the twelve [18] and while they were reclining at table and eating, Jesus told them, "Truly I tell you one of you will betray me, one of you eating with me." [19] They started to be distressed and one by one they said to him, "No way it's me, is it!"

[20] He said, "It's one of the twelve dipping into the bowl with me. [21] The Son of Man goes as it is written about him, but woe betide that man by whom the Son of Man is betrayed! It would be better for him if he'd never been born."

Thinking about Mark

Jesus' actions in the temple and his critique of the temple establishment put him on a collision course. Mark portrays the chief priests and scribes as determined to silence him for good. In the events that follow, Mark alternates the episodes between those that bring something negative and those that bring something positive. The first episode is negative: it reports the plot to kill Jesus (14:1–2). Then comes a positive episode: the response of a woman (14:3–9). There follows Judas' initiative to betray him (14:10–11), and on the narrative goes, alternating negative and positive.

In the week before Passover Jerusalem filled with pilgrims. The crowds made it possible for Jesus to get away with actions such as his acclaimed entry and his causing a disturbance in the outer court of the temple. The potential for unrest in the assembly of so many people was high, and both the temple authorities and the Roman authorities would need to jump on disturbances as quickly as possible and get rid of anyone likely to cause trouble. Jesus would have been seen as one of them.

Mark moves from the negative and threatening, regarding the betrayal of Jesus (14:1–2), to the positive when he reports the incident in Bethany (14:3–9). It takes place in the house of Simon the leper, presumably now cleansed, but nevertheless suggesting that Jesus found support among marginalized people. A woman anoints Jesus with a jar of costly ointment. The story appears to have circulated widely and to have attracted numerous expansions as people tried to make sense of it. At its simplest it is an anecdote according to which a woman approached Jesus and expressed her affection and Jesus accepted it.

Her unusual action clearly raised questions. Nothing in Mark's story suggests she was a sinner, but what was going on and why did Jesus allow her to do this? Some would have expected Jesus to stop her. Nothing suggests it was a sexual advance, despite such massage oil being used by prostitutes, but better be safe, many would have thought, and not allow anything that might seem shameful. Should Jesus really accept such an expression of appreciation from a woman like that? Mark's story suggests that the men present were not comfortable.

Mark has those men—presumably, as Matthew indicates, including his disciples—complain about the waste, especially when the money from the sale of such a jar of oil, nearly a year's wages' worth, could have been given to the poor. Mark has Jesus tell them to leave her alone, suggesting that there is always a need to help the poor but that opportunity to show affection to him was only for a limited time. He then has Jesus declare that she had done what she could, add that the anointing was for his burial, and that her act would be remembered across generations of his followers.

Matthew repeats the story (26:6–13) but has the disciples as the ones who complain. John's Gospel also knows the story but locates it before Jesus' entry into Jerusalem and identifies the woman as Mary, sister of Martha and Lazarus who live in Bethany (12:1–8). That makes it more respectable. It knows the complaint that selling it would raise nearly a year's wages' worth of money, which could be given to the poor, but has the complaint raised now by Judas Iscariot, not the others. Jesus' response is similarly to leave her alone, to refer to the poor as being always in need and to say that this was an anointing for his burial. There are, however, significant differences. Apart from identifying her as Mary and having Judas make the complaint, it has Mary apply the oil not to Jesus' head but to his feet and wipe them with her hair.

Even more complex is Luke's version, which appears to be a separate variant. He omits telling it where the others place it, near the end of Jesus' life, and instead places it much earlier (7:36–50). It still takes places in the house of a man called Simon, but here he is not a leper but a Pharisee. The woman comes with her box of oil, as in Mark, yet anoints not his head but, as in John, his feet and also weeps over them. That marks another significant difference: she is a known sinner. Many, hearing Luke's story, might have imagined that her sin was sexual promiscuity or even prostitution, given the oil, which is possible, but Luke does not say so. Others later speculated that it was Mary Magdalene, also not something Luke suggests. Against the Pharisee's shock that Jesus allowed such attention, Luke has Jesus defend it as gratitude for forgiveness.

The story has done the rounds, being told and retold, embellished and expanded. Does Luke's version make her action more acceptable? Was she originally a person of doubtful status, easily described as a sinner? Was it the mere fact that she was a woman that made the men uncomfortable? How far was the complaint about waste a way of avoiding that reality? Does John make her acceptable by identifying her as one of Jesus' good friends? Was the original action an anointing of Jesus' feet, in John perhaps foreshadowing Jesus' washing his disciples' feet? Is Luke right that the event belonged earlier in Jesus' ministry? Did Mark place it at the end because he wanted to interpret the anointing in relation to burial? Was the detail of her anointing Jesus' head, not his feet, an attempt to suggest his being the Anointed One, the Messiah?

We may never know the answer to many of these questions. It must have made an impact that Jesus went against social norms to allow the event to happen. In that sense, it was typical of his tendency to cross norms and boundaries in embracing divine compassion as entailed in the good news. Whether the placement is his own or had already been set by his tradition, Mark makes a connection between the story and Jesus' death, suggesting that the act could be seen as foreshadowing his burial.

By contrast to this positive episode, Mark goes on to report Judas' initiative to betray Jesus (14:10–11). Details are minimal. We next hear of Judas arriving with temple authorities in Gethsemane to make the arrest (14:43–45). Judas' action has generated much reflection, from people seeing him acting with goodwill to provoke Jesus to take assertive action, to people seeing him as a profoundly evil man. Matthew takes up the motif of payment and connects it with Zechariah's mention of the thirty shekels of silver, thrown into the treasury (11:12–13), suggesting that the authorities gave Judas thirty pieces of silver (Matt 26:15). He later reports Judas' throwing the silver into the temple and committing suicide by hanging (27:3–10). Luke in Acts offers a more gruesome scene: Judas buys a field but then "falling headlong, he burst open in the middle and all his bowels gushed out" (Acts 1:18). Matthew has the field bought instead by the temple authorities, but both explain that this is why it came to be called "The Field of blood."

From the negative, Mark turns again to the positive, the preparation for Jesus and his disciples to celebrating the Passover (14:12–16). According to Mark, followed by Matthew and Luke, Passover was on the Friday, and by Jewish reckoning, commenced Thursday evening after sundown. The Passover meal came, therefore, at the beginning of Passover Day, our Thursday evening, and Jesus was tried and then executed on the Friday, still Passover day. John's Gospel differs. It has Jesus die when the Passover lambs were slain but also sees this as happening on the Friday, but has Passover day take place on the Saturday, the Sabbath, also commencing at sundown the night before. Was John thereby engaging in symbolism or was Mark in making Jesus' last meal, forerunner of Holy Communion, a Passover meal? We may never know for sure.

Mark's account of Jesus sending off two disciples with instructions on how to find the suitable room recalls his sending two disciples to get the donkey. Good planning or something miraculous? Mark does not suggest the latter but may have implied it.

The negative turn (14:17–21) comes with the scene of Jesus and the twelve already seated in the room and Jesus' reporting about his impending betrayal by one of them. Mark may intend his hearers to attribute Jesus' knowledge to miraculous powers but does not say so. It may be implied, as is the notion that Jesus' betrayal in some way fulfills scripture: "The Son of Man goes as it is written about him, but woe betide that man by whom the Son of Man is betrayed! It would be better for him if he'd never been born" (14:21). The "woe" may express sadness; it probably expresses anger, such as in Mark's time his hearers would feel hurt and anger when betrayed. It has the potential to turn to hate.

In Mark's account Jesus does not specify Judas as the culprit, in contrast to John's Gospel, where Jesus tells the beloved disciple it is Judas (13:24–26), and in Matthew where Judas has Jesus confirm that he is the one (26:25). Only John mentions that Judas left the twelve after being identified, but even then, the others, he suggests, had no idea of what he was about to do, thinking that, as the one with the purse, Jesus had sent him off to purchase something (13:27–30). The other canonical gospels assume he had departed from them at some point and would reappear at the arrest in Gethsemane. None indicates his absence during Jesus' symbolic acts with the bread and wine.

Reflection: What indicates that the woman's approach to Jesus was seen as a problem and what attempts do we see to manage it? Can she be a model? Can Judas be a model?

Final Meal (14:22–25)

Listening to Mark

²² And while they were eating, he took a loaf of bread and having blessed it, broke it up into pieces and gave it to them and said, "Take, this is my body." ²³ And taking a cup of wine and giving thanks, he gave it to them, and they all drank from it. ²⁴ And he said to them, "This is my blood of the covenant poured out for many. ²⁵ Truly I tell you, I won't be drinking of the fruit of the vine anymore until that day when I drink it new in the kingdom of God"

Thinking about Mark

Mark's story assumes that Jesus' final meal with his disciples was well underway when Jesus initiated his actions. "While they were eating," he spoke of betrayal (14:18). Now again Mark says: "while they were eating" (14:22). Having spoken of the Passover meal, we may also assume that this took place within the context of the Passover meal, but Mark gives us no further detail about that special meal. Nothing suggests that Jesus' action was an adaptation, let alone an adoption of the meal for his own purposes.

Instead, he simply has Jesus take a loaf of bread, bless and break it open, much as otherwise a father might do in introducing a meal, the equivalent of saying grace. Jesus' words of invitation to his disciples, "Take; this is my body," have generated reams of speculation. What did he mean? Was he claiming to have changed its substance in some literal sense? Was he focusing on his physical flesh? Neither seems likely. At its simplest, it meant: This is me. I am sharing myself with you.

In the context of impending death, the breaking could foreshadow his being broken, in that sense, in his death and mean: "This is my body broken for you," but we would need to read that into the text. It is not there. In the context, this act indicates that in his life and his death he has given himself to them and for them. The other version of the event, preserved in Paul's letter to the Corinthians, has Jesus say: "This is my body that is for you. Do this in remembrance of me" (1 Cor 11:24).

The Passover meal included more than one point where wine was shared. Again, Mark makes no specific connection, but instead simply says that Jesus took a cup, presumably filled it with wine, again gave thanks, and shared it with his disciples who all drank from it. Sharing from one cup of wine is a way of indicating oneness and solidarity. This then comes to the fore in his words: "This is my blood of the covenant poured out for many" (14:24).

Again, Mark does not mean us to think of a magical transformation of wine to become Jesus' blood, nor to see Jesus singling out his blood in a literal sense. As in our use of the word bloodshed, blood stands for death. Jesus is saying something about his death and in doing so relating it to the notion of covenant. Some might have thought of a covenant sacrifice, which celebrated an agreement or resolution. The words, "for many," point to Jesus' death as going to benefit more than just the disciples.

Alongside the sense of togetherness with his own, communion, there is also the implicit claim that his death will bring benefit for many. The only other place where Mark has Jesus say anything comparable is in his statement that he would give his life as a ransom for many (10:45). Ransom, as we noted, was not meant in a literal sense, but reflected a wider use of the image to express something that makes liberation possible. One of the widely held interpretations of Jesus' death was that far from being a disaster and defeat, it did what the deaths of martyrs had also done. It produced a surplus of goodness, which brought benefit by way of forgiveness for others.

Mark has Jesus speak of his death as having such an impact, unleashing grace and forgiveness for all open to receive it. Matthew spells this out by having Jesus add this specifically: "This is my blood of the covenant, which is poured out for many for the forgiveness of sins" (26:28). We might see it as Jesus' life and his going so far as death as making a declaration of God's love and forgiveness for all, which in shorthand form can be summarized in the words: Christ died for us or for our sins.

That can help us make sense of what in their world entailed assumptions that we no longer share in the same sense. These include that the death of a righteous person covers or makes up for more than his own sins but extends to ensure forgiveness for others. Related notions included speaking of Jesus' death as doing what sacrifices were believed to achieve: namely releasing positive influence that compensated and cleansed.

Those who press the imagery more literally can go on to see Jesus as offering himself as a substitute, to take the punishment that others deserve and so pay their debt, indeed, even as settling accounts with God and so enabling God to love and forgive. Such literal interpretations frequently depict God in ways that run contrary to the way Jesus himself portrayed God, namely, as reaching out in generosity and love, offering forgiveness and not demanding someone must take the due punishment before he could do so. Such was already John the Baptist's understanding and was upheld and repeated by Jesus during his ministry. Forgiveness was always at the heart of Israel's faith.

Mark concludes his account of Jesus' actions by having him set what he was doing in the light of the great vision of future hope as a great feast, something that had been central to his ministry. In that sense his action was a foretaste of what was to come, solidarity celebrated, and also affirmed a goal: "I won't be drinking of the fruit of the vine any more until that day when I drink it new in the kingdom of God" (14:25).

Matthew takes up Mark's account with the addition about sins, but also by having Jesus directly speak the invitation in relation to the wine as well as the bread: "Take, eat; this is my body" is matched by "Drink from this, all of you; for this is my blood of the covenant, which is poured out for many for the forgiveness of sins" (26:28–29), a neater balance and more fitting for liturgical use. It is characteristic of Matthew to make such stylistic improvements in taking up Mark's material. It was natural once these two actions were brought together as a unit for the wording to be made to correspond. We reenact them quite independently of a meal and at Corinth it is clear that they followed a meal (1 Cor 11:20–21). This was apparently not always so.

Unlike Mark and Matthew, Paul and Luke's accounts indicate that between the sharing of the bread and the cup is a meal. Both refer to his taking the cup after the meal (1 Cor 11:25; Luke 22:20). The two acts were not together, as in Mark and Matthew. Paul's version, our earliest, and Luke's will have preserved the earlier practice.

Having the bread before the meal, like the saying of grace, and the cup at the end of the meal, might also explain why Paul or his tradition saw no need to make Jesus' words match, as in Matthew: "This is my body" and "This is my blood." It also helps us to see that the focus in Paul's version is not on having food, as though we should think of the substance of the bread and the wine, because people were already eating the drinking in a meal.

The focus is more on the actions of the sharing. Paul mentions the event primarily to use it to address a failure to understand its meaning and the meaning of the gospel in Corinth, which has to include sharing and caring also for the poor and is emptied of its meaning if some people come to it hungry while others come having been well fed (1 Cor 11:20–22).

In relation to the bread, Paul has the words, literally: "This is my body [that is] for you" and to the wine: "This cup is the new covenant in my blood" (11:25). The allusion to the "new covenant" probably stands under the influence of Jeremiah: "The days are surely coming, says the LORD, when I will make a new covenant with the house of Israel and the house of Judah" (31:31). We may read between the lines that the intent is to indicate that an ancient hope is being fulfilled, perhaps in a way which Mark expresses differently when he has Jesus speak of the coming kingdom. In the context in Jeremiah the fulfillment is that the law is to be written on people's hearts, but this is not taken up by Paul, though it would cohere with the way he sees liberation.

Mark's words, which simply refer to "my blood of the covenant" may allude to Zechariah: "the blood of my covenant" (9:11) or to Moses's words to the people on their agreeing to keep the law: "See the blood of the covenant that the LORD has made with you in accordance with all these words" (Exod 24:8). Neither allusion is particularly evident, so that the focus appears rather to be on involvement together in a new or renewed relationship with God.

Paul's version, echoed in part by Luke, who combines Paul's and Mark's version, includes the words: "Do this in remembrance of me" after each sharing of the bread and the cup. It adds a dimension of the past beside the sense of future hope and present oneness or communion.

Luke's version (22:14–23) emphasizes more closely the fact that the context was a Passover meal and that it points forward to the time when he would eat with them in the kingdom of God. He then takes a cup and makes a similar comment about not again going to drink wine with them until they would do so in the kingdom of God. Only after that does Luke have Jesus take the bread and say the words, "This is my body, which is given for you. Do this in remembrance of me," as in Paul's version, and then take a second cup after the meal and say, "This cup that is poured out for you is the new covenant in my blood," a combination of what we find in Paul's version and what we find in Mark's. There were multiple cups in the Passover liturgy. Luke has Jesus use two of them.

All four versions emphasize Jesus' giving of himself for others and the way that the meal foreshadows the hope he embraces, so often depicted as a great feast to which all were invited, so that to engage in communion together in remembering him was at the same time to engage in communion in committing oneself to that vision of inclusivity.

Reflection: How can we say Jesus died for our sins and also say that he and John the Baptist and Israel's faith already affirmed divine forgiveness? What message does Holy Communion bring to us about the past, the present, and the future?

THE END?

Denial and Trial (14:26-72)

Listening to Mark

²⁶ Having sung a hymn, they departed for the Mount of Olives. ²⁷ And he says to them, "All of you are about to fail, because it is written, 'I shall strike the shepherd and the sheep will be scattered,' ²⁸ but after I am raised up, I will go ahead of you to Galilee." ²⁹ Peter said to him, "Even if all are going to fail, I won't." ³⁰ Jesus said to him, "Truly I tell you, today this very night before the rooster crows twice you will deny me three times." ³¹ He countered strongly, "Even if I have to die with you, there's no way I am going to deny you." And the others all expressed the same sentiments.

³² And they come to the place called Gethsemane and he says to his disciples, "Sit here while I pray." ³³ And taking Peter and James and John with him, he began to be distressed and troubled. ³⁴ And he told them, "I'm terribly sad enough to die. Stay here and keep alert." ³⁵ So he went a bit further on and fell on the ground and prayed that if it were possible the hour might pass him by ³⁶ and he said, "Abba, Father, all things are possible for you. Take away this cup from me; but what matters is not what I want but what you want." ³⁷ Then he returned and found them asleep and so he says to Peter, "Simon, you're sleeping? Couldn't you keep awake for just one hour? ³⁸ Stay alert and pray, so you won't end up being put to the test. The spirit is willing, but the flesh is weak."

³⁹ So again he went off to pray along the same lines as before ⁴⁰ and again returned to find them asleep, because they could hardly keep their eyes open, and they didn't know what to answer him. ⁴¹ So he comes back a third time telling them, "Sleep on and rest up; that'll do. The hour has come. See, the Son of Man is being betrayed into the hands of sinners. ⁴² Get up, let's go. Look the betrayer has arrived."

⁴³ And immediately while he still speaking Judas, one of the twelve, arrives and with him a crowd with swords and clubs from the chief priests and the scribes and the elders. ⁴⁴ The betrayer had given

them a sign saying, "Whoever I kiss, he's the one. Grab him and lead him safely away." ⁴⁵ So he came straightaway and approached Jesus, addressing him with the words, "Rabbi" and kissed him. ⁴⁶ They laid hands on him and seized him. ⁴⁷ One of those standing there drew his sword and struck the high priest's slave, cutting off his ear. ⁴⁸ Jesus' response was to say, "Have you come after me like I'm a brigand with swords and clubs to arrest me? ⁴⁹ I was teaching in the temple day after day and you didn't arrest me, but ok, let the scriptures be fulfilled."

⁵⁰ And all the rest abandoned him and fled. ⁵¹ And a certain young man was a follower, wearing just a linen garment over his naked body, and they got hold of it ⁵² and he let the linen garment go and ran away naked.

⁵³ And they brought Jesus to the high priest and all the chief priests and elders and scribes gathered together. ⁵⁴ Meanwhile, Peter followed from afar up into the courtyard of the high priest and was sitting there with the attendants and warming himself by the fire. ⁵⁵ The chief priests and the whole council sought evidence against Jesus in order put him to death but weren't finding any. ⁵⁶ For many gave false testimony against him and their evidence was contradictory. ⁵⁷ Then some got up and gave further false evidence against him, saying, ⁵⁸ "We heard him say, 'I shall destroy this temple made with hands and in three days build another one not made with hands,'" ⁵⁹ but still, their evidence was contradictory.

⁶⁰ Then the high priest got up in their midst and questioned Jesus, saying, "Why aren't you responding to what these people are accusing you of?" ⁶¹ He stayed silent and gave no response. So again, the high priest asked him, "Are you the Messiah, the Son of the Blessed?" ⁶² Jesus replied, "I am. And you will see the Son of Man sitting at the right hand of power and coming with the clouds of heaven." ⁶³ The high priest tore his robe and said, "Why do we still need more evidence? ⁶⁴ You have heard his blasphemy. What do you think?" They all condemned him as deserving death. ⁶⁵ And some started spitting at him and covered up his face and punched him, saying, "Prophesy!" And the attendants knocked him about.

⁶⁶ Now while Peter was downstairs in the courtyard, one of the women attendants of the high priest approached him ⁶⁷ and, noticing him warming his hands, looked at him and said, "You were with Jesus the Nazarene, too." ⁶⁸ He denied it and said, "Nope, I don't know the

guy and I don't know what you're talking about." And he went off into the foyer area. ⁶⁹ And the woman attendant saw him go and started saying to those nearby, "He's one of them." ⁷⁰ But he denied it. Then a short while later those nearby said to Peter, "You really are one of them and you're Galilean." ⁷¹ He started to curse and swear, "I don't know this guy you're talking about." ⁷² And immediately the rooster crowed a second time and Peter remembered the word that Jesus had said to him, "Before the rooster crows twice you will deny me three times" and he collapsed in tears.

Thinking about Mark

Mark's story is about Jesus, but it is also about the disciples. What would it be like to be a disciple in Mark's time and be listening to his account? You have just heard of Jesus speaking to his apostles about giving his all, then of the conclusion of their time together with a hymn and their heading back to the Mount of Olives together. And there, Jesus announces that they are all to be failures and desert him when he faces death (14:26–27). He cites Zechariah: "I will strike the shepherd, and the sheep will be scattered" (Zech 13:7). How shocking! Perhaps also very disturbing if some of Mark's audience had experienced or contemplated being hauled up before the authorities. Was Mark deliberately evoking such awareness?

No, I won't, protests Peter, and the others join him. Jesus fatefully predicts Peter will deny him not just once but three times before the local rooster has even crowed twice. Mark will go on to show the prediction proved true and by morning Peter had done just that (14:66–72). Shame! Failure! Mark offers some relief from the apparent hopelessness by having Jesus add that after his resurrection he would go before them to Galilee (14:28). We have to wait till the very last verses of Mark's account to see this going to be fulfilled. Mark's hearers would know that this event lifted Peter and the others back up out of the hole they had dug for themselves through their fear and failure. This hope will have helped Mark's hearers endure what happened next without feeling entirely overwhelmed.

It was not as though Mark was about to portray a brave Jesus, triumphantly battling adversity unmoved and untouched, a hero in contrast to his disciples' weakness. Instead, in the scene in Gethsemane, he portrays a very troubled Jesus engaging his fear and distress, a real Jesus just like them

(14:32–36). He took his inner circle with him, Peter and James and John, this time not to see a glorious vision but a man feeling broken, throwing himself on the ground. Pathetic, undignified!? One widely attested variant in Luke's account of the scene speaks of his sweat as like great drops of blood falling to the ground (22:44). The Letter to the Hebrews appears also to know the story and speaks of Jesus pleading with loud cries and tears to God to save him (5:7).

By contrast, John's Gospel, which prefers to show Jesus more in control, has him say to himself: "Now my soul is troubled. And what should I say—'Father, save me from this hour'? No, it is for this reason that I have come to this hour" (12:27). Mark has no such compunction. He has Jesus pray that God would save him from such suffering: "Abba, Father, all things are possible for you. Take away this cup from me; but what matters is not what I want but what you want" (14:36), expressed similarly in Matthew and Luke.

Jesus' determination not to give up at the last minute and retreat from danger came at a deep cost to him. Mark's hearers would know that and would sense the shame that his very inner circle failed to stay with him despite his returning to them three times. Storytellers often favored recounting events in sets of threes and that is playing a role here as it was in the prediction that Peter would deny three times. It was also a way of underlining the depth of failure on the disciples' part.

Jesus' words on his first return, having confronted Peter, address all three, but Mark's hearers would surely hear themselves addressed: "Stay alert and pray, so you won't end up being put to the test. The spirit is willing, but the flesh is weak" (14:38). They might well have known the words of the Lord's Prayer, "Do not bring us to the time of trial" (Matt 6:13). Matthew recognizes this and adds to Jesus' prayer: "your will be done" (26:42, echoing 6:10). Mark already had Jesus issue the call to the disciples to stay awake, in his closing address to them (13:32–37).

Their failure is in a sense compounded when one of their own, Judas, arrives on the scene with the temple police to arrest Jesus: "a crowd with swords and clubs from the chief priests and the scribes and the elders" (14:43). John's version adds "soldiers," reflecting likely involvement from the Roman authorities. Identifying Jesus by a kiss is not as shocking as it may sound to those of us in social contexts where men do not usually greet each other in that way.

THE END?

A disciple fighting back sword in hand (14:47)? It seems so. Mark has Jesus challenge the arresting party for approaching him like he was a militant, emphasizing that he was a teacher. Matthew adds a rebuke of the disciple, reflecting awareness of the need for more direct distancing of Jesus and the movement from anything military or subversive, characteristic of what most hope for from a messianic movement (26:52–54). Such would have been a red rag to the Roman authorities, both in Jesus' time and also in later decades, who saw the movement anyway as subversive, even if not by sword but by word.

Before he reports the trial of Jesus before the high priest, Mark has Jesus alert his hearers to scripture fulfillment. Jesus had cited Zechariah as predicting that the disciples would abandon him and now, he reports, they do: "And all the rest abandoned him and ran away" (14:50). One young man who fled escaped naked because his pursuers stripped him of the scant linen cloth he was wearing. Mark may well be referring to a known figure but offers us no clue. Sometimes authors built themselves into their storytelling. We may never know. A young man also appears in the empty tomb—could it be the same one? Mark does not say.

Mark has Jesus brought to the high priest and the council, the Sanhedrin, which included chief priests, elders, and scribes, and slips in a reference to Peter entering the high priest's courtyard (14:53–54). To have such a council meeting at night, let alone on Passover day, was highly irregular, but Mark gives no indication of being aware that this was so. Luke, who must have known, transfers the actual trial at least to the next morning (22:66–71). John's Gospel, which on some of the historical details appears more accurate, mentions only a hearing with the former high priest, Annas, and then with Caiaphas, the high priest at the time, but no trial (18:19–24). Mark or his tradition may have assumed more than that.

In Mark's version of events the council struggles initially to find sufficient evidence to warrant a death sentence, something they had no authority to carry out, so it would have to be done by the Roman authorities at their request. Mark reports what he rightly suggests was a false claim, namely, that Jesus had said: "I shall destroy this temple made with hands and in three days build another one not made with hands" (14:58).

Mark's hearers know that Jesus had indeed predicted the temple's destruction, but not by his own hands. John's Gospel knows a version of the saying, which it puts on the lips of Jesus, but which begins not "I shall destroy" but simply "Destroy," namely referring to others responsible for the destruction (2:19). It is highly likely that Jesus' challenge to the temple establishment by word and action was seen as subversive, not only by the temple establishment but also by the Roman authorities, who saw themselves as protectors and controllers of the temple. They depended on its personnel for keeping the land stable, and that included through its financial role as virtually the land's bank. Mark's tradition preserves awareness of the offence Jesus' words and actions were considered to be.

The partially false allegation of Jesus' attack on the temple and its establishment finds an echo in the word uttered by those ridiculing him as he hung on the cross: "Ha! You who were going to destroy the temple and rebuild it in three days, save yourself and come down from the cross!" (15:30). In another of Mark's sets of threes, a third reference comes when the destruction is symbolically fulfilled as the temple's curtain is torn apart from top to bottom (15:38).

The other primary accusation and the one that the council finally forward to Pilate is the charge that Jesus was a would-be Messiah, a charge not unrelated to his action with regard to the temple, as we have seen. In Mark's version, which emphasizes Jesus' silence, the high priest asks him directly: "Are you the Messiah, the Son of the Blessed One" (14:61). "Son of God" was one of the titles for a king and so for the hoped-for king of David's line, but was nevertheless much more than just an honorific title. It was how God had addressed him at his baptism (1:11) and spoken of him at his transfiguration (9:7). He was Messiah, so also Son of God, but in a very different sense from what was popularly assumed and he was certainly not the leader of a revolutionary movement wanting to fight the Romans. Luke separates the question into two because being Messiah was one thing, and being the Son of God was, in his mind, a much bigger thing (22:66–71).

Mark has Jesus say, yes, he was the Messiah, but then shift the language, as he had done before when accepting Peter's acclamation, to speak of himself as the Son of Man. Mark has Jesus adopt the understanding of messiahship that we see, for instance, in the Parables of Enoch (1 Enoch 37–71), where the Messiah/Son of Man figure acts on God's behalf to rescue God's chosen ones and judge others: "you will see the Son of Man seated at the right hand of the Power, and coming with the clouds of heaven" (14:62). The language is inspired by the vision in Daniel that depicts a human figure, one like a son of man, coming on the clouds of heaven and entrusted with God's kingdom (7:13–14).

Nothing in this claim amounts to blasphemy, although later claims by subsequent generations that Jesus was the Son of God would be understood as claiming divinity for him and would be seen as amounting to blasphemy. Some of Mark's hearers may have faced or heard of trials before synagogue authorities, where this charge was laid. Mark may have patterned the trial on the basis of such later trials and accusations. John, who knows no such trial, but just a hearing, nevertheless agrees at least that the charge forwarded to Pilate was the claim to messiahship (18:33). Mark has Jesus, the prisoner, abused by those present and then beaten by the temple guards (14:65), typical of the brutality of the time and also of other times under authoritarian regimes.

Mark had briefly mentioned Peter as he began his account of the trial. He now has Jesus' prediction come true about him just as he did with the prediction about the disciples fleeing like sheep when their shepherd was attacked (14:66–72). Shame, Peter! He is broken, but that is not the end. Perhaps some of Mark's hearers knew the experience of failure, themselves, or knew of such failure by others.

Reflection: What does Mark mean us to see as false and what as true in Jesus' saying about the temple? What might it mean to watch in today's world?

Crucifixion (15:1–39)

Listening to Mark

^{15:1} Straightaway, first thing in the morning, the chief priests called for a consultation with the elders and scribes and the whole council and bound Jesus and took him off and handed him over to Pilate. ² So Pilate interrogated him, "Are you the King of the Jews?" He replied, "You say so." ³ And the chief priests were leveling many allegations against him. ⁴ So Pilate asked him again, "Why aren't you responding? Look what they are accusing you of." ⁵ But Jesus kept on not saying anything in response, so that Pilate was amazed.

⁶ Now at the festival he used to release for them one prisoner whom they could ask for. ⁷ And there was one called Barabbas, imprisoned with the rebels who had committed murder in the uprising. ⁸ So the crowd came up and started asking that he do for them what he usually did. ⁹ Pilate responded to them, saying, "Do you want me to release for you the King of the Jews?," ¹⁰ knowing that the chief priests had handed him over because they were envious of his influence. ¹¹ But the chief priests stirred up the crowd, to ask rather that he release Barabbas to them. ¹² Pilate again responded to them, saying, "What then do you want me to do with the King of the Jews?" ¹³ They again shouted out, "Crucify him!" ¹⁴ Pilate said to them, "Why—what evil has he done?" But they shouted out all the more, "Crucify him!"

¹⁵ Pilate, wanting to do right by the crowd, released Barabbas to them and handed Jesus over to be flogged and crucified. ¹⁶ The soldiers took him inside the courtyard, called the praetorium, and brought together the whole military unit. ¹⁷ And they dressed him up in purple and twisting some thorny twigs into a crown, put it on his head ¹⁸ and started addressing him, "Hail, King of the Jews!" ¹⁹ And they hit him on the head with a reed and spat on him, and falling to their knees, bowed before him.

²⁰ And when they had finished ridiculing him, they removed his clothes and took him away to crucify him. ²¹ And they commandeered

Simon of Cyrene, the father of Alexander and Rufus, on his way in from the countryside, to carry his cross. ²² So they bring him to Golgotha, which means the place of a skull, ²³ and offered him wine mixed with myrrh, which he turned down, ²⁴ and they crucified him and divided up his clothes by casting lots who should take what.

²⁵ It was the third hour when they crucified him ²⁶ and the statement of what he was charged with read, "The King of the Jews." ²⁷ And along with him they crucified two brigands, one on his right, and one of his left. ²⁹ And people passing by slandered him shaking their heads and saying, "Ha! You who were going to destroy the temple and rebuild it in three days, ³⁰ save yourself and come down from the cross!" ³¹ Likewise, the chief priests with the scribes mockingly said to one another, "He saved others, but he can't save himself. ³² Let the Messiah, the king of Israel, come down now from the cross so we can see and believe," and those crucified with him also reviled him.

³³ And at the sixth hour darkness came over the whole land until the ninth hour. ³⁴ And at the ninth hour Jesus cried out with a loud voice, *Eloi eloi lema sabachthani?*, which in translation is, "My God, my God, why have you forsaken me?" ³⁵ And some standing nearby, when they heard it, said, "He's calling for Elijah." ³⁶ So someone ran and filled a sponge with wine, put it on a reed, and offered him a drink, saying, "Let's see if Elijah will come and take him down?" ³⁷ But Jesus, uttering a loud cry, breathed his last, ³⁸ and the sanctuary curtain was split in two from top to bottom. ³⁹ The centurion standing opposite him, when he saw how he expired, said, "Truly this man was God's Son."

Thinking about Mark

Mark has the council meet a second time in the morning. Luke makes that the occasion for the trial (22:66–71) and so omits the meeting in the middle of the night, which would have been highly unlikely, and John, as noted, had no Jewish trial, just a hearing. What does appear in common in the diverse accounts is that Jesus was brought before Pilate and with the charge that he was a would-be Messiah, a "King of the Jews."

The charge of being a would-be Messiah, a "King of the Jews," appears to have been attached to his stake at the crucifixion. From a Roman perspective, it is understandable. Stability on the eastern flank of the Empire was very important. Unrest was not to be tolerated. Any movement that looked subversive, whether by force of arms or force of words, belonged in the category of subversion and was to be seen as an enemy of Roman governance. As noted above, this would include anyone threatening the temple, for which the Romans stood as protectors. In none of the accounts does it surface, however, as a Roman concern in dealing with Jesus.

The charge of being a would-be Messiah was enough for the Romans to come down hard on Jesus. Pilate must have been made aware that Jesus' was not a militia movement because we hear of no attempt to round up his followers. Mark's account reflects the assumption that Jesus was seen as a leader of subversion. This explains why we hear of the offer of a swap for another subversive, Barabbas, and why Jesus was crucified between two other subversives.

It is highly unlikely that Mark or his tradition had access to a detailed report of Jesus' trial before Pilate. This is why we have considerable variety in reconstruction of what must have been said and done. Common to all is the basic charge and there is no reason to doubt its historical veracity. Much beyond that is reconstructive imagination of the kind expected of serious historians and biographers of the day.

The imaginative reconstruction might well explain why Mark has Jesus remain silent throughout most of the ordeal whereas John has him engage in dialogue. It probably also explains other aspects, such as Pilate showing some admiration and also the hostility of the temple establishment and the crowd.

Some accounts, such as that of Matthew, go almost so far as to exonerate Pilate of responsibility, having him wash his hands in innocence (27:24), and having the Jewish crowd take on responsibility ("His blood be upon us and our children"; 27:25), including for the disaster and slaughter of people during the 70 CE capture of Jerusalem and the destruction of the temple, depicted as divine punishment. Sadly, John's Gospel has the awful irony of the Jewish leaders declaring that they had no king but the emperor, a denial of the heart of their faith (19:15). Much of this sentiment now coloring the accounts reflects tensions between early Christians, including Christian Jews, and the synagogue, and the ways, healthy and unhealthy, that some sought to process their hurt and anger.

Mark's account of the trial is brief and focuses on the charge. His account of Pilate's offer to swap Jesus for Barabbas (15:6–15) is the occasion for emphasizing the role of the Jewish leaders and the crowd. The name

Barabbas means "Son of the Father," which raises the suspicion that something other than history is at work here.

The abuse, now at the hands of soldiers (15:16–20), is again typical of the brutality of autocratic regimes, but also may underline ironically the claim: ridiculed for who he really was, the "King of the Jews," but just not as popularly understood.

The account of the crucifixion, itself (15:21–32), is also a mix of reality, historical reconstruction, and interpretive reflection. The reality was that he was indeed put to such a shaming death, hung on a cross. Crucifixion was a deterrent, warning passersby of the consequences of such crimes against the state. Some debate whether the charge was nailed above him, but it is certainly possible. There is no reason to doubt that he was put in the category of a subversive, reflected in those crucified with him. A ghastly painful ordeal. That is how it was meant to be. Rome crucified thousands of such people.

Was there a personal memory passed on by the children of a man on his way into the city who was asked to carry Jesus' cross, Simon of Cyrene, the father of Alexander and Rufus, when in his physical state Jesus failed to do so himself (15:21)? Possibly, otherwise, suggesting such a memory would have made little sense. Mark's hearers must have known of them.

Some other detail may be imagined or added in the light of descriptions of suffering in the Psalms. Psalm 22 was a key source, where we find the following: "They divide my clothes among themselves, and for my clothing they cast lots" (22:18); "All who see me mock at me; they make mouths at me, they shake their heads; 'Commit your cause to the LORD; let him deliver—let him rescue the one in whom he delights!" (22:7–8); and "My God, my God, why have you forsaken me?" (22:1).

Did these verses from the Psalm 22 generate the details in Mark's story or were they brought to the details secondarily? The former seems more likely. Mark fills out the mockery with a set of three insults. Passersby allude to his statement about destroying the temple: "Ha! You who were going to destroy the temple and rebuild it in three days, save yourself and come down from the cross!" (15:29–30). The chief priests and their associates refer to his claim to be the Messiah: "He saved others, but he can't save himself. Let the Messiah, the king of Israel come down now from the cross so we can see and believe" (15:31–32). Even those on either side of him mocked him.

Mark frames the events around three sets of three hours. Crucifixion at the third hour (9 am); darkness over the land for three hours from midday; and then Jesus' final death at the ninth hour (3 pm). The imagery of darkness is symbolic. Mark's scene is simple. He has Jesus call out in the words of Psalm 22:1, which some mistakenly hear as calling for Elijah, the figure expected to accompany the Messiah. He then cries out and expires (15:33–37).

Mark does not glorify the event. It was a real death. He does however give it color not only by painting it as a moment of deep darkness, but as also a moment that brought fulfillment of his prediction of the temple's destruction with the tearing of its curtain. Significantly, he then has not a disciple or another Jew but a gentile soldier, seeing how he died, declare: "Truly this man was God's Son!" (15:39). This is the third of three acclamations, the first two being given by God at his baptism (1:11) and at his transfiguration (9:7). The tearing of the curtain might remind some of the tearing open of the heavens that precede the first acclamation, and some have seen more, such as symbolism of opening a way to God.

What might the centurion have understood? Was he simply impressed by Jesus' noble suffering? Luke re-jigs his words to express simply that he thought Jesus was an innocent man (23:47). Mark is likely to make him symbolic of the gentile response to the gospel that he has sought to emphasize.

Mark's account is relatively simple. Jesus is dead, killed on false grounds as being in the category of would-be Messiahs. He dies as an innocent, suffering like the righteous before him have suffered, and so he is portrayed using images and words drawn from Psalm 22. There is nothing here reflecting the image of the suffering servant of Isaiah 53, which inspired later thought. No symbolic earthquakes and breaking open of tombs, as in Matthew (27:51–54). No embellishments to reassure hearers that the death was real, issuing blood and water when pierced by a soldier or to assure succession of the witness by Jesus' entrusting his mother to the care of the beloved disciple, the would-be authority behind John's Gospel (19:34–37). Jesus died.

Reflection: On what grounds did Pilate crucify Jesus? Why did he not round up the disciples and kill them, too? In what sense does following Jesus today pose a challenge to political powers?

THE END?

Resurrection and Renewal (15:40—16:8)

Listening to Mark

⁴⁰ And there were women there, looking on from a distance, among whom were Mary Magdalene, Mary the mother of James the younger and of Joses, and Salome. ⁴¹ They were followers from when he was in Galilee and cared for him. And there were many other women who had accompanied him to Jerusalem.

⁴² When it was already late in the day, since it was the day of preparation before the Sabbath, ⁴³ Joseph of Arimathea, a respected nobleman, who was someone harboring hopes for the kingdom of God, dared to approach Pilate and ask for the body of Jesus. ⁴⁴ Pilate was amazed that he was already dead and summoned the centurion to ask him whether he had been dead long. ⁴⁵ When he heard from the centurion, he then allowed Joseph to take the body. ⁴⁶ So, buying linen cloth, he took him down, wrapped him in linen cloth, and put him in a tomb that had been carved out of a rock, and closed up the entry to the tomb with a stone.

⁴⁷ Mary Magdalene and Mary the mother of Joses saw where he had been put. ¹⁶:¹ So once Sabbath had passed, Mary Magdalene, Mary the mother of James, and Salome bought spices to go to the tomb to anoint him. ² And very early on the first day of the week they come to the tomb at sunrise. ³ They were discussing among themselves, "Who will roll away the stone from the entry to the tomb?" ⁴ But when they looked, they saw the stone had already been rolled away, because it was really quite large.

⁵ So they enter the tomb and see a young man sitting there on the right-hand side, wearing a white robe, and they were alarmed. ⁶ He said to them, "Don't be alarmed. You're looking for Jesus the Nazarene who was crucified. He is risen. He's not here. Look, there's the place where they put him. ⁷ But now, go and tell his disciples and Peter that he's going on ahead of them to Galilee and you'll see him there, as he told you." ⁸ So they left and fled the tomb, because they were scared and stunned, and said nothing to anybody because they were afraid.

FOLLOWING MARK

Thinking about Mark

After reporting Jesus' death, Mark makes a point of referring to women who had observed his fate. He names some of them: "Mary Magdalene, Mary the mother of James the younger and of Joses, and Salome" (15:40). He will mention them again shortly in reporting their visit to Jesus' tomb to attend to his body in the tomb (16:1).

The male disciples had presumably fled. Mark alerts his hearers not only to the willingness of these women to stick with Jesus, at least at a safe distance, but also that they had been playing an important role in the movement, fulfilling what was a traditional gendered role of being providers for the welfare of the group, as in a family. They with others had made the journey from Galilee to Jerusalem with him. This affirmation of their role and their belonging, even if in traditional terms, signals an assumption about their inclusion and would have been reassuring for women hearing the account. They were not deemed not worth naming or mentioning, but were being valued in their own right.

We know nothing of Joseph of Arimathea, the council member, other than what Mark tells us (15:42–46). It was plausible that some in high positions were sympathizers, but for their own protection were deft in not making it known. Mark offers no judgment on his lack of open support, but we might imagine not all would have viewed it positively. His act was to avoid having Jesus hanging on the cross all Sabbath day, when actions such as taking him down would have been deemed a breach of Sabbath law, and when his body would have been exposed to such indignities as birds pecking his face and dogs tearing at his legs. It was kind and caring.

Mark's story that he retrieved the body by approaching Pilate assumes his status in the establishment, as does, presumably, his possessing or having access to a tomb. Such tombs were not left open, so closing it reflected standard practice at one level, but prepared for the drama shortly to come. Might there have been senior people among Mark's hearers who would have taken heart from Joseph's act? It could, after all, have cast suspicion on him and put him in danger.

Two of the three women just mentioned, Mary Magdalene and the other Mary, had seen the location of the tomb (15:47) and so, once Sabbath was over and the sun was up, all three approached his tomb to ensure the body was properly laid out and smeared with oil and spices, as was the custom. Mark narrates what happened very simply. They wondered how they could roll away the stone cover, which we may assume would have been hard for them to move, but to their surprise they found the tomb open (16:1-4).

The drama continues when they then enter the tomb and see a young man sitting on one side, dressed in a white robe, who sensed their alarm. After all, he might have removed the body or someone might have stolen it. He has the final word in Mark's Gospel, reassuring them that Jesus had been raised and instructing them: "Go and tell his disciples and Peter that he's going on ahead of them to Galilee and you'll see him there, as he told you" (16:7). Astonishingly, Mark then reports that the women were so terrified they fled and "said nothing to anybody" (16:8).

This is such an unusual ending to his gospel that many have wondered if there was once more, which has gone missing. We know that some manuscripts, though not the best ones, add some verses to round off the work. It is, however, likely that Mark really did end his gospel in 16:8. It raises many questions. Mark's final note that the women failed to comply and tell the disciples may be a way of helping explain why the story of the women emerged late in the piece and was not an early tradition.

Mark is clearly aware of stories about Jesus appearing to Peter and then to others in Galilee and implies that he and the others had simply returned home and had not been given the young man's instructions. Our earliest account of what happened, namely the one cited by Paul, also reflects this understanding. He writes: "For I handed on to you as of first importance what I in turn had received: that Christ died for our sins in accordance with the scriptures, and that he was buried, and that he was raised on the third day in accordance with the scriptures, and that he appeared to Cephas [Peter], then to the twelve" (15:3-5).

Neither that early account nor Mark mentions an appearance first to the women, as in Matthew (28:9-10), or just to Mary Magdalene, as in John's Gospel (20:11-18). That appears to be a secondary addition as people engaged in creativity and imagination about what happened, including stories of earthquakes and angels descending to roll away the stone, and one sitting atop it and giving the instructions (Matt 28:1-4), or of Mary Magdalene rushing off to tell the disciples who are assumed to be in Jerusalem, and Peter and the beloved disciple racing to the tomb to see for themselves (John 20:1-10).

The simple attribution of faith in Jesus' resurrection being based on an appearance to Peter in Galilee appears also to be reflected in what the eleven disciples told the two who had met Jesus on the road to Emmaus when they returned to Jerusalem as the basis for their belief in Jesus' resurrection: "The Lord has risen indeed, and he has appeared to Simon [Peter]!" (Luke 24:34).

Mark's story assumes that, in the events that followed, the disciples would have returned to Jerusalem, where history's climax was expected to take place, and, either in Galilee or there, made connection with the women who then told the story of the empty tomb. Alternatively, the story Mark tells of their finding the tomb empty may be what people believed must have happened and so wrote it up that way, together with the angel figure or the young man.

It was not unthinkable, given their understanding of resurrection, that people, might have imagined that Jesus could appear in places as far apart as Jerusalem and Galilee. For while they assumed that resurrection entailed raising the corpse, they also assumed that it was not a resuscitation, but a transformation of the body into a spiritual body which had the ability to appear and disappear, a distinction that Paul makes clear to the Corinthians about resurrection bodies: "It is sown a physical body, it is raised a spiritual body" (1 Cor 15:44).

When Matthew and Luke rewrite Mark's account they exhibit the authorial freedom typical of symbolic stories. Matthew introduces an earthquake into the story, an angel descending from heaven to roll the stone away and sit on it, the guards at the tomb stunned to lifelessness, and the women carrying out the angel's instructions and so telling the disciples, and then even having their own encounter with the risen Jesus (28:9).

Luke has two angels encounter the women in the tomb, give them the same instructions, which they follow, telling the skeptical disciples, but then has Peter rush off to the tomb, also finding it empty (24:4–12). John's Gospel has only Mary Magdalene at the scene and arriving before dawn (20:1, 11–18). It makes no mention of angelic intervention but has her rush off to tell the disciples in response to which Peter and the beloved disciple race each other to the tomb, with the beloved disciple the winner, symbolic of the author's claim to superior understanding of Jesus (20:2–10). Whereas in Matthew Jesus encounters the women, in John he encounters only Mary Magdalene.

Mark offers us no explanation about why Jesus' resurrection was important. The earlier debate with the Sadducees showed that belief in future resurrection was not a novel idea. We have to look elsewhere to understand that, to begin with, it was God saying yes where Pilate and others said no.

THE END?

It demonstrated that Jesus was right in what he proclaimed. That was why people understood his resurrection as the beginning of the end times when all would be raised and why they appear to have returned to Jerusalem where it was all meant to happen and to which he would return very soon as royal Messiah. Grief and loss turned to gain and action.

Mark's account has another puzzle: is the young man dressed in white an angel or is he connected to the young man inserted earlier into the narrative of the fleeing disciples, the young man who fled naked having had his skimpy loin cloth ripped off (14:51–52)? Is this Mark again saying something about himself and his gospel, namely that he knows the true story of Jesus? We began by saying that we will never find Mark in his gospel. Have we now found him? We may speculate, but we will never know.

Reflection: What effect did belief that God raised Jesus from the dead have for the first disciples? How would it have affected the way they saw the past, the present, and the future? How much of this can be meaningful for us today?

What Now after Listening to Mark?

How might the first hearers of Mark's Gospel have reacted to his account? How might Mark have wanted them to react? To answer these questions requires an exercise in imagination but also in drawing out the implications of what Mark clearly valued.

The story did not end in defeat. It was more then than a heroic tragedy. And while Jesus at the end is transported into a different dimension of reality, what he started remains. At the very least, his resurrection indicated that God affirmed who he was and what he was doing. That is also much more than vindication of the past because he also entrusted his work and hope to others and Mark and Mark's listeners were their successors. The Jesus story is more than an exercise in historical curiosity. It has existential relevance for them.

If we asked them, then, what does it mean for you, one of their answers would be to reaffirm the hopes that Jesus expressed. Mark has Jesus say that very soon—indeed, within a generation and certainly very soon after the disaster of the temple's destruction in 70 CE—history would reach its climax: Jesus himself would return with his angels and gather them to safety with him. It would be hard to imagine that this would not have been a key take from the story, even if from our perspective nearly two millennia later, it cannot bear the weight it had for them.

Alongside this, indeed, seen as an essential component in being ready for it, was the commission to continue Jesus' mission. Jesus did not call disciples to establish a fan club to adore him. He gathered disciples to do what he did. Mark makes it clear that this entailed reaching out into the community to bring healing and restoration. They would have continued to understand healing within the framework of demonology and so as expelling demons by various means, inspired and enabled to do so by the Spirit. In that sense, they, too, were to do what John said of Jesus: to baptize with the Spirit. Again, from our perspective two millennia later, healing remains a core concern. While we no longer see it within the framework of demonology, as they did, we share the view that healing is liberating people from what oppresses them.

Not only would Mark's original audience have taken seriously that they inherited Christ's commission, but they would also have looked to what it meant by seeing what Jesus did. That included not just various forms of healing but also a willingness to reach out with acceptance to people often shunned because of their sometimes deserved reputation of being exploiters. They would also have taken on board Jesus' flexible way of interpreting the commandments by making love and compassion central.

Furthermore, they would also have appreciated confirmation of their own status as belonging to the largely gentile branch of the movement, seeing the way Mark symbolized their inclusion twice: first, by pairing the healing of the gentile Gerasene demoniac with the Jewish girl aged twelve and the woman with a twelve year hemorrhage and second by pairing the two major feedings, one of five thousand Jews and one of four thousand gentiles, on either side of Jesus' teaching about setting traditional barriers rooted in biblical provisions aside.

They very likely would have understood Jesus' last meal as inaugurating what was now their practice of sharing bread and wine to celebrate their belonging together, as well as remembering Jesus and embracing the hope the meal foreshadowed of the coming great feast. In that context Mark has intimated that Jesus' death was a significant self-giving with liberating effects which assured forgiveness. Mark does not elevate that motif to become the major message of the gospel, as if to render the details of Jesus' ministry of no particular significance, as one might read Paul and even the later creeds. Mark clearly does not see his account as in that sense redundant as far as the gospel is concerned and as merely a matter of historical interest. Jesus and his one-year ministry was the good news as much as any interpretation of his death. The two belonged together.

Mark's first hearers might well have been struck by how he portrays the disciples. His audience needed to take on board that if those first disciples were so fallible, they, too, could fall into the same trap. For them it might still be falling into the trap of ambition, failing to see where love leads, and projecting onto Jesus and God the obsessions with status and power that were dominant in their society and remain dominant in ours.

Jesus' suffering and death would have been more than something to reflect on from a distance. For some it was what they were probably experiencing or could potentially experience. They would need each other. They needed to stay awake. They needed to be good news for the poor, inclusive of children, embrace both men's and women's roles as they then saw them, and seek to sustain stable marriages and households.

And so they would have begun to listen to Mark's Gospel, perhaps initially at one sitting, since it is not very long, but then as excerpts read alongside their Bible, the Greek Old Testament, and perhaps copies of other writings from their movement, such as letters of Paul. Mark was clearly convinced that the story was worth retelling and had relevance for the ongoing cause. He must have convinced many, who even made copies and shared them widely.

Matthew and Luke highly valued his work and took it as their basic framework as they tried new attempts to depict Jesus' significance and the author of the Fourth Gospel seems at least to have some knowledge of Mark's work and perhaps of the others when engaging in his freely creative and inspiring portrait of Jesus as God's word incarnate, mirroring the divine with claims to represent its light, life and truth, and its nourishment as the true bread and living water, much more even than tradition had attributed to the divine law and wisdom.

What now? Their answers inspire while also seeming for us in some respects remote and alien, not least their demonology and their assumptions that they were in the end time. Our connection embraces their hope, still rich in its vision of justice and peace, but without their timing. We can affirm their theology of God's reign and way as one of bringing liberation and inclusion, but not defined in demonology and the cultural norms of their world. Our cross-cultural encounter with Mark and his world leaves us with both a sense of great distance and a sense of proximity. As twenty-first-century audiences, we hear a voice that calls us to embrace this gospel's hope and liberation in solidarity and to find oneness in being inspired by its story.